CHILDREN'S MINISTRY THAT WORKS!
The Basics & Beyond

Edited by Jolene L. Roehlkepartain

Loveland, Colorado

Children's Ministry That Works!
The Basics & Beyond
Copyright © 1991 by Group Publishing, Inc.

Second Printing, 1992

Credits
Edited by Jolene L. Roehlkepartain
Cover and interior designed by Jill Christopher
Illustrations by Andy Robertson
Cover photo by Jeff Buehler

Data from *Effective Christian Education: A National Study of Protestant Congregations* are used with permission from Search Institute, 122 W. Franklin Ave., Ste. 525, Minneapolis, MN 55404, 800-888-7828. All rights reserved.

Scripture quotations are from the Holy Bible, New International Version. Copyright © 1973, 1978, 1984 International Bible Society. Used by permission of Zondervan Bible Publishers.

Library of Congress Cataloging-in-Publication Data
Children's ministry that works! : the basics & beyond / edited by Jolene
    L. Roehlkepartain.
        p.   cm.
    Includes bibliographical references.
    ISBN 0-931529-69-7
    1. Church work with children. 2. Christian education of children.
I. Roehlkepartain, Jolene L.
BV639.C4C44 1991
259'.22—dc20   91-21680
                                                            CIP

Printed in the United States of America

CONTENTS

Part One: Children's Ministry Foundations

Chapter 1: Beyond Babysitting: Children's Ministry Today...........11
By Jolene L. Roehlkepartain

Children's Ministry Programs • Teachers and Leaders • The Pastor's Role • Children's Ministry Materials • Children's Needs • A Vital Ministry • In-Depth Information: Children's Ministry Emphases • In-Depth Information: Children's Programs Churches Offer • In-Depth Information: Materials Children's Ministers Use

Chapter 2: Children Today: It's a Tough World After All 23
By Jolene L. Roehlkepartain

Complex Family Situations • Stress • Accidents • Drugs • Abuse • Poverty • Homelessness • Ministering to Children's Needs • In-Depth Information:The Boom in Drug-Infested Babies • In-Depth Information: Drugs and Alcohol—Churches Mum on the Subject

Chapter 3: Leadership That Lasts.....................................35
By Judy Wortley

Characteristics of a Good Volunteer • The Basics of Recruitment • How to Train Volunteers • Leading Monthly Training Sessions • Working With Volunteers • In-Depth Information: Searching for Volunteers • Creative Idea: Getting People Talking

Chapter 4: Getting Parents on Board................................45
By Paul E. White, Ph.D.

Importance of Parental Involvement • Getting Parents Involved • An Alternative: Family Sunday School • Providing Help for Parents • Ministering to Single-Parent Families • A Parenting Ministry • In-Depth Information: Parents' Experiences When They Were Children • Creative Idea: Building Relationships With Parents

Part Two: Teaching Techniques

Chapter 5: Learning by Doing..**55**
By Terry Vermillion

What Is Active Learning? • Children Learn in Different Ways • Doing Active Learning • Making the Bible Come Alive • Active Learning in Children's Ministry • In-Depth Information: 7 Learning Styles • Worksheet: Choosing an Active-Learning Activity

Chapter 6: Great Games for Kids..**67**
By Terry Vermillion

Competitive and Non-Competitive Play • Choosing Games • Games for Young Children • Games for Elementary-Age Children • Creative Idea: Dealing With Competition • In-Depth Information: Choosing Games for Different Ages

Chapter 7: Adventurous Art and Creative Crafts............................**75**
By Mary Gray Swan

The Importance of Art and Creativity • Doing Art With Children • Essential Art Materials • Organizing Your Art Supplies • Art With a Conscience • Age-Appropriate Arts and Crafts • Creative Idea: Colorful Adhesive • Money-Saving Tip: Easy Art Supply Recipes • In-Depth Information: Crafts for All Ages

Chapter 8: Making Music With Children...**85**
By Margaret Rickers Hinchey

Music Helps Children Express Their Faith • Everyone Can Be Musical • Creative Music Ideas • Leading Children's Music • Making Music Fun for Children • Creative Idea: Making Music With Preschoolers • In-Depth Information: Meaningful Music for All Ages

Chapter 9: Presentations With a Purpose.......................................**93**
By Dale and Liz VonSeggen

Puppets With a Purpose • Secrets of Storytelling • Ministering With Clowns • Drama: The Dramatic Teacher • Illusions: Memorable Presentations • Daring to Be Creative • Money-Saving Tip: 5 Inexpensive Puppet Stages • Creative Idea: Storing Puppets •

Money-Saving Tip: Transform Garbage Into Storytelling Props • Creative Idea: Using Hats and Masks in Storytelling • Worksheet: Planning a Creative Presentation

Part Three: Age-Specific Ministries

Chapter 10: The Power of Prenatal Ministry **109**
By Vicki Ashcraft

Why Minister to an Unborn Child? • The Benefits of a Prenatal Ministry • Elements of Prenatal Ministry • Ministry in Problem Pregnancies • Recruiting Volunteers • The Children's Ministry Foundation • In-Depth Information: Parenting Starts at Conception • In-Depth Information: The Job Description for a Prenatal Partner • Worksheet: The Prenatal Partner Agreement

Chapter 11: Giving Your Nursery Rhyme and Reason **117**
By Jean Cozby

Essentials of an Effective Nursery • Nursery Necessities • Laying a Spiritual Foundation • Staffing Your Church Nursery • Making Your Nursery a Success • Worksheet: Safe Nursery Checklist • In-Depth Information: Nursery Discipline • In-Depth Information: Teenage Nursery Workers

Chapter 12: Discovering the World With Preschoolers **125**
By Mary Irene Flanagan, C.S.J.

Understanding Preschoolers • How to Give Preschoolers a Spiritual Foundation • Making God Real to Preschoolers • Making Religious Holidays Meaningful • Learning By Experience • Creative Idea: Getting to Know Your Preschoolers • Creative Idea: Photogenic Walls • Worksheet: Evaluating Your Preschool Program • Creative Idea: A Prayer Preschoolers Can See

Chapter 13: The Exciting World of K-3 ....**133**
By Vince Isner

Their Bodies • Their Minds • Their Senses • Their Spirits • Their World • In-Depth Information: Different Kids; Different Paces

Chapter 14: The Changes and Challenges of
Upper Elementary **141**
By Dan Wiard

Physical Changes • Intellectual Changes • Other Changes • Sixth-Graders: Where Do They Fit? • The Best Issues to Study With This Age Group • How Do We Keep Them Coming? • Interest Kids Now; They'll Be Back Later • In-Depth Information: Fifth- and Sixth-Graders' Top Worries • Worksheet: How Well Is Your Program Working?

Part Four: Children's Ministry Programs

Chapter 15: Meaningful Programs for Children............................**151**
By Earl Radford

Before Starting a Program • Starting New Programs • Financially Supporting Your Programs • Scheduling Children's Ministry Programs • Planning a Special Event • The Special Event Countdown • Meaningful Programs • Worksheet: Program Planning

Chapter 16: Sunday School From Start to Finish **159**
By Barbara Younger and Lisa Flinn

Setting Up Classrooms • Choosing Curriculum and Resources • Using Creative Teaching Methods • Preparing a Lesson • Teaching the Lesson • Ending a Class • Evaluating Your Teaching • Worksheet: Curriculum Evaluation Checklist • In-Depth Information: Teaching Age-Appropriate Activities • Money-Saving Tip: Fantastic Flannel Boards • In-Depth Information: Handling Behavior Problems

Chapter 17: Innovative Children's Church................................**173**
By Rick Chromey

The Need for Children's Church • Types of Children's Churches • Four Pillars of a Children's Church • Elements of a Successful Children's Church • Organizing a Children's Church • Measuring Your Success • In-Depth Information: Child-Adult Ratios for Children's Church • Worksheet: Rate Your Children's Church

Chapter 18: Worship With the Whole Church.............................**181**
By Wes Haystead

The Challenges of Worship • Effective Ways to Include Children in Worship • Planning a Meaningful Service • Worksheet: Evaluate Your Worship Service • Creative Idea: After-the-Service Talk Tips

Chapter 19: Adventures in Vacation Bible School.....................**191**
By Mitchell Picard

Rethinking Vacation Bible School • 10 Creative VBS Themes • Vacation Bible School Ingredients • Planning Your Vacation Bible School • What Starts When VBS Ends • Worksheet: Vacation Bible School Registration Card • Creative Idea: Encouraging Kids to Bring Their Friends • Creative Idea: Attracting VBS Volunteers • Worksheet: A Vacation Bible School Checklist

Chapter 20: Successful After-School Programs...........................**199**
By Elaine Friedrich

Step 1: Determine the Need • Step 2: Determine Your Program's Purpose • Step 3: Plan, Plan, Plan • Step 4: Choose a Focus • Step 5: Decide Who Can Participate • Step 6: Set a Regular Schedule • Step 7: Develop a Transportation Plan • Step 8: Find Committed Leaders • Step 9: Evaluate Your Program • Worksheet: After-School Child Care Questionnaire • In-Depth Information: Kids With Nothing to Do After School

Chapter 21: Special Ministries for Special Needs **207**
By Wayne Tesch

Child Abuse and Neglect • Hospitalized Children • Developmentally Disabled Children • A Touching Ministry • Creative Idea: 10 Ways to Brighten a Hospital Stay • In-Depth Information: Mentally Disabled Children • Worksheet: Test Your Ministry Readiness • In-Depth Information: Helpful Organizations

Appendixes

Children's Developmental Stages and Needs..............................**215**
Resources for Children's Ministry...**219**
Contributors **225**

Part One:
Children's Ministry Foundations

CHAPTER 1

BEYOND BABYSITTING: CHILDREN'S MINISTRY TODAY

■ ■ ■ ■ ■ ■ ■ ■ ■ ■ ■ ■ ■ ■ ■ ■

BY JOLENE L. ROEHLKEPARTAIN

The door to the education building of an Arkansas church has two doorknobs. One is for adults. The other—18 inches lower—is for children. The church doesn't need a sign that says "Children are important here." It shows that attitude in everything it does. You're just as likely to be handed a bulletin by an 8-year-old as by an adult when you attend the church's worship services.

● ● ●

Frustrated by few volunteers and dismal attendance in vacation Bible school, a church in Georgia changed its format. Instead of the traditional weeklong program, it started a once-a-week vacation Bible school that lasted all summer. Not only did the new format attract more children to the church, it increased the church's visibility in the community.

● ● ●

"I believe that attracting young families, those with preschool- and school-age children, especially, is vital to church growth," says a staff member at a growing church in Kansas. "Strong children's and youth ministries are a plus for families looking for a church home."

● ● ●

Churches are rediscovering children. They're learning, once again, the importance of providing solid, creative programs for children. They're searching for helpful ways to respond to the changing needs and problems of children. And they're learning that a solid children's ministry invigorates the church's whole ministry.

A solid children's ministry program is a key drawing card for people looking for a church. According to sociologist Wade Clark Roof of the University of California, Santa Barbara, the biggest group of church dropouts now returning to church is married couples with children.[1]

Ninety-six percent of church members and 73 percent of people who don't attend church say they want their children to get religious training, says a Princeton Religion Research Center study.[2] These people are looking to the church—and especially the church's children's ministry—to give their children that religious training.

So how are churches doing?

Children's Ministry Programs

When Search Institute surveyed about 10,000 people in 493 churches, it found that churches do well in many aspects of children's ministry (which the study categorized as programs for children in grades one to six).[3] Eighty-five percent of Christian education directors say their churches' children's ministry programs are "good" to "outstanding."

According to the study, 82 percent of Christian education directors say it's "very true" that the classes and children's ministry events feel warm and inviting. Three out of four say it's "very true" that the children enjoy the children's ministry program.

Other strengths of the children's ministry program that Christian education coordinators identified include:

● It promotes growth in religious faith—61 percent

IN-DEPTH INFORMATION

Children's Ministry Emphases

Search Institute surveyed Christian education directors about how much they emphasized 22 different topics in their overall children's ministry.

Five Topics Strongly Emphasized
1. Teaching Bible stories.
2. Developing Bible knowledge.
3. Teaching moral values.
4. Learning how to apply faith to everyday life.
5. Providing fellowship or social interaction.

Five Topics Not Emphasized or Emphasized Slightly
1. Providing classes to help parents learn how to promote the faith of their children.
2. Informing parents of students' progress.
3. Discussing local or national issues.
4. Providing classes for parents on effective parenting or communication.
5. Awareness and understanding of other faiths' traditions.

—J.R.—

● The annual children's ministry budget is carefully planned—60 percent

● Space for children's ministry education is adequate—56 percent

● It's well-planned and administered—54 percent

● It addresses children's needs and interests—53 percent

● It challenges children to think—51 percent

In contrast to these strengths, the study also found weaker aspects of children's ministry. Only 45 percent of Christian education directors say it's "very true" that their programs are innovative. And only 34 percent say it's "very true" that churches do much to encourage participation of inactive children.

Though most churches aren't innovative, churches that do innovate meet important needs. At St. Matthew Lutheran Church of Fort Worth, Texas, 3- to 8-year-olds make quilts for foster babies. The group also buys "going home" outfits for these foster babies.[4]

When the interdenominational church, Washington (D.C.)

IN-DEPTH INFORMATION

Children's Programs Churches Offer

So what do churches offer in children's ministry programming? According to Search Institute, the percentage of churches that offer:
- Sunday or church school for kindergartners—99 percent
- Sunday or church school for kids in grades 1-6—99 percent
- Sunday or church school for pre-kindergartners—98 percent
- Vacation Bible school—90 percent
- Children's sermons during worship—78 percent
- Children's choir—74 percent
- Leadership training for Christian education volunteers—57 percent
- Church-related nursery—48 percent
- Discussion or seminars for parents—37 percent
- Youth group activities for fifth- and sixth-graders—31 percent
- Church-related day care—19 percent
- Church-related after-school program—13 percent[5]

—J.R.—

Community Fellowship, asked the community what the church should be doing, the people said "tutor our kids." So the church does just that. Each day 30 kids come to the Neighborhood Learning Center to work on their homework and get individual help from tutors.[6]

First Baptist Church of Topeka, Kansas, updated its entire Sunday school program. "I was pulling out materials that were dated 1948 or 1963," said church member Pam DeFries about the Sunday school curriculum. "Our methods were very antiquated. Young people are used to the latest, the most modern, the most innovative approaches in the public schools. The church should be contemporary too."

Now the church has computers, a large-screen television, video equipment, puppet theaters, Bible dolls and lots of activities for the children to learn about God during Sunday school. Children actually participate in the learning instead of just listening to what's being taught.[7]

Teachers and Leaders

Although Christian education directors rate their overall children's ministry programs well, they're not as optimistic about the teachers and leaders who work directly with the children.

Only 29 percent of Christian education directors in the Search Institute study say it's "very true" that teachers and leaders know educational theory and practice. Only one out of three Christian education directors (and 29 percent of teachers themselves) say it's "very true" that teachers know about different learning styles. And only 24 percent say it's "very true" that teachers know and understand the theology and traditions of the church's denomination.

In other aspects of educating children, Christian education directors rank their teachers' skills higher than the teachers do, which may indicate that Christian education directors need to be more in touch with their teachers and volunteers. Christian educators ranked their teachers higher in these four areas than the teachers did:

● Teachers deal well with conflict.
● Teachers know how to minimize discipline problems.
● Teachers have teaching competence.
● Teachers enjoy participation.

Teachers lack self-confidence. They need to learn appropriate teaching skills. They need support. They need practical ways to deal with disruptive behavior. And they need affirmation and encouragement.

One positive finding of the Search Institute study is that nine out of 10 Christian education directors say it's "very true" that their teachers are caring and loving—an essential attribute needed in children's ministry, especially since so many children feel unloved.[8]

This important trait in leaders can have a tremendous impact on children. Patrick Whaley, a children's minister in Tennessee, tells about a fifth-grade boy in his church who, for the second time in a week, had run away from home. Whaley found the boy's Sunday school teacher, and together they drove up and down streets looking for Jake.

At midnight, unsuccessful and discouraged, they drove to the church. They noticed the light was on in the fifth-grade classroom. When they investigated, they found Jake asleep on the carpet.

"Jake! Jake! We've been looking for you!"

Jake stirred and opened his eyes. "Mr. Watkins. Mr. Whaley. This is the place where I feel loved."

Eleven years later, Whaley received a letter from Jake, who was working in Korea. "I remember many lessons I learned at church," Jake wrote, "and how people loved and accepted me. Thank you for taking time with me and giving me a chance."[9]

The Pastor's Role

The senior pastor sets the congregation's priorities. If the pastor makes children a priority, the church will too. But if the pastor doesn't take the children's ministry seriously, neither will the congregation.

Consider the priority of children's ministry in one Texas congregation where the pastor's openness and leadership in children's ministry set the mood for the congregation. Children feel comfortable sitting in the pastor's lap. In fact, a fifth-grade girl wanted to plan a worship service without any help from the pastor or other adults. She felt that the church cared enough about children that people would appreciate the effort—even if everything didn't go smoothly.

In general, how do Christian education coordinators rate their senior pastors in supporting the church's children's ministry? According to the Search Institute study, 78 percent of Christian education directors say it's "very true" that their pastors are knowledgeable about the theory and practice of educating children.

Christian education directors also speak highly of the pastor's commitment to children's ministry. Seventy-four percent say it's "very true" that the pastor shows a deep commitment to the Christian education of children. And 71 percent say it's "very true" that the pastor is enthusiastic about educating children.

But actions speak louder than words. Although Christian education directors speak highly of the pastor's commitment, they don't give the pastor high marks when it comes to practice. Only 42 percent of Christian education directors say it's "very true" that the pastor helps in educating children.

Pastors don't rate themselves highly when it comes to actually participating in Christian education with children. According to Search Institute, 43 percent of pastors say they haven't spent any time within the past month participating in Christian education with 6- to 12-year-olds. Another 28 percent of pastors say they had spent only one hour in the past month educating these kids.

This lack of time may reflect that many pastors don't enjoy helping with children's Christian education. Only 13 percent of pastors say they enjoy participating in Christian education "a great deal" with children age 3 to 5. The percentage doesn't rise much in Christian education of elementary-age kids. Only 16 percent of pastors like being involved in Christian education "a great deal" with 6- to 12-year-olds. Yet 63 percent like participating in Christian education "a great deal" with adults.[10]

Children's Ministry Materials

Donna Brandt, who taught elementary school for 12 years, recently evaluated 58 different curricula from a variety of Christian publishers across the country. In many ways, her findings were discouraging. She writes: "Finding good Sunday school curriculum is no easy task. There's a lot out there, and children will probably hear about God's love through most lessons. But as I evaluated the curriculum, I asked myself, 'Would children really learn, enjoy and experience the lesson?' In many cases, I decided the answer was no."[11]

The quality of resources churches use is a key to effective children's ministry. Interestingly, Christian education directors rank children's ministry materials much higher than teachers who use the resources. When asked whether quality children's curriculum resources are available, 80 percent of Christian education directors say "very true," whereas only 66 percent of teachers do.

Another material dispute evolves around multi-media resources. Fifty-one percent of Christian educators, but only 39 percent of teachers say it's "very true" that quality multi-media resources exist.

Furthermore, few churches offer a good library or resource center for children's ministry workers. Only 37 percent of Christian education directors and 35 percent of teachers say it's "very

IN-DEPTH INFORMATION

Materials Children's Ministers Use

About three out of five Christian education directors say they rely primarily on denominational materials for their children's ministry curriculum. The following chart shows the percentage of churches that use these types of materials by age, according to Search Institute.[12]

Curriculum resource	Kinder-garten	Grades 1 & 2	Grades 3 & 4	Grades 5 & 6
Denominational	60%	62%	62%	60%
Nondenominational	11%	10%	10%	10%
Other denominational resources	11%	9%	10%	10%
A combination of denominational and other denominational resources	7%	8%	7%	7%
A combination of denominational and nondenominational resources	6%	6%	5%	6%
Other resources	5%	5%	6%	7%

—J.R.—

true" that a quality Christian education library or resource center is available.[13]

Children's Needs

If someone asked you the needs and interests of the children in your church, what would you say? Would you know? Where would you get your information?

The Search Institute study found that churches generally do little to identify then meet the specific needs of their children. Fifty-nine percent of Christian education coordinators said they hadn't done a survey of their children's needs and interests within the past year.

Similarly, most churches rarely ask children themselves to help plan their programs. In fact, 66 percent say children have never participated in planning the children's program in the past year. Although developmentally children aren't ready to plan and administer a Sunday school class or after-school program, their input of what activities they like to do can give vital clues to their needs and interests.

Every church, every community is different. How can you know what the important issues are in your congregation if you don't ask? Children in your area may grapple with very different issues than children in Manhattan, New York, or Manhattan, Kansas. To find out the needs of your children and the issues they're dealing with:

● **Talk to parents.** In fact, try to visit children's families in their homes. You may be surprised to find families living in poverty. Find out if your children are in blended families, single-parent families, two-income families, families where unmarried couples live together, families going through a separation or divorce, or other difficult family situations. Ask the parents what issues they're facing with their children.

● **Listen to the children.** Give children time to talk spontaneously about what *they* want to talk about. You can often do this when you're eating a snack with the children or giving them quiet time.

● **Visit your public school.** Talk to elementary teachers. Ask the administration for community demographics. Most schools track the changes in the community.

● **Have children vote.** Make a list of concerns that you feel your children may be dealing with. During one of your programs, have children vote on issues they're worried about by raising their hands. Or talk individually to children. Often the question, "What question do you wish you had the answer for?" will stimulate a lively response. Older children, those in fourth- to sixth-grade, can take anonymous, written, needs surveys.

A Vital Ministry

Once you identify the needs and interests of children in your church, you can develop a children's ministry kids won't be able to resist. A children's ministry should lay a Christian foundation for children. It can only do that if churches focus energy, creativity and careful thought on making children's ministry a first-class, important ministry—so that people see it as *real* ministry, not just babysitting.

Children's Ministry That Works! gives you the practical guidance you need to develop an innovative, creative ministry that will make a difference in children's lives. It's divided into the following sections:

● **Children's Ministry Foundations**—This section explores key foundations of working with children, including understanding children today, recruiting and training leadership, and working with parents. These chapters help you build a support structure for your ministries.

● **Teaching Techniques**—In this section, you'll get hands-on advice about teaching techniques and how they work with children. Plus, you'll find dozens of creative active-learning, craft, music and presentation ideas.

● **Age-Specific Ministries**—Since a newborn is very different from a sixth-grader, this section explains key needs, issues and concerns in working with each age—from prenatal through sixth grade.

● **Children's Ministry Programs**—This final section gives you step-by-step guidance for establishing and fine-tuning various children's ministry programs, including Sunday school, after-school programs, special events, vacation Bible school, and programs for children with special needs.

Our children live in a tough world. They need the best the church can offer to help them establish a firm foundation for adolescence and adulthood. In order to minister to children, we need to understand their world and the issues they face. That is the focus of the next chapter.

Notes
■ ■ ■ ■

[1]Kenneth L. Woodward, "A Time to Seek," Newsweek (December 17, 1990), 50-56.

[2]*The Unchurched American . . . 10 Years Later* (Princeton, NJ: Princeton Religion Research Center, 1988), 35.

[3]Peter L. Benson and Carolyn H. Eklin, *Effective Christian Education: A National Study of Protestant Congregations, A summary report on faith, loyalty, and congregational life* (Minneapolis: Search Institute, 1990), 5-6.

[4]"Fostering Care for Children," The Lutheran (January 9, 1991), 23.

[5]Unpublished data from *Effective Christian Education: A National Study of Protestant Congregations.*

[6]"Tutoring and TLC," World Vision (April/May 1990), 16.

[7]Laura Alden, "Can Sunday School Reclaim Center Stage?" The American Baptist (September 1990), 17.

[8]Unpublished data from *Effective Christian Education: A National Study of Protestant Congregations.*

[9]Patrick Whaley, "Where's Jake?" CHILDREN'S MINISTRY Magazine (March/April 1991), 23.

[10]Unpublished data from *Effective Christian Education: A National Study of Protestant Congregations.*

[11]Donna Brandt, "The Best & the Worst Sunday School Curriculum," CHILDREN'S MINISTRY Magazine (May/June 1991), 10.

[12]Unpublished data from *Effective Christian Education: A National Study of Protestant Congregations.*

[13]Ibid.

CHAPTER 2

CHILDREN TODAY: IT'S A TOUGH WORLD AFTER ALL

■ ■ ■ ■ ■ ■ ■ ■ ■ ■ ■ ■ ■ ■ ■ ■

BY JOLENE L. ROEHLKEPARTAIN

It isn't easy being 3. Or 5, or 8 or 11. Children today deal with many tougher, more serious issues than kids did 20 years ago. "The concept of childhood, so vital to the traditional American way of life, is threatened with extinction in the society we have created," writes David Elkind in his book *The Hurried Child*. "Today's child has become the unwilling, unintended victim of overwhelming stress."[1]

For too many kids, this is not the age of innocence.

● Seven-year-old David wanted to open a lemonade stand to raise money so his family could move. His family lives in a homeless shelter.

● Three-year-old Shawntea is sick with the nation's most common serious childhood disease. If she doesn't get better soon, her brain will be damaged. Shawntea is suffering from lead poisoning; she eats peeling plaster off her bedroom wall.

● Ten-year-old Ricky was missing. His parents feared he'd been kidnapped. Ricky's parents later learned that Ricky and his friends had been playing "chicken" in an abandoned grain silo by jumping from one conveyor belt to another. Ricky lost his balance and fell to his death.

● On her second birthday, Sarah ran in front of the television that her dad was watching. Her 6-foot-tall, 225-pound father rose from his chair and punched the 2-year-old in the stomach so hard she fell to the floor.

● From the time she was in the womb, Jeanne had the odds stacked against her. Jeanne's mother abused drugs while she was pregnant, and after a difficult delivery, Jeanne spent the first three years of her life withdrawing from heroin.

● Once an outgoing, happy child, 6-year-old Hilary became withdrawn. She began throwing temper tantrums. A child therapist finally pinpointed the problem. Hilary's parents had gotten a divorce, and Hilary was upset that her mother's boyfriend slept over three times a week.

● By age 4, Christopher could speak three languages fluently: English, Swedish and Spanish. He took violin and karate lessons and attended a school for gifted children. But Christopher had trouble sleeping. He got headaches and often became irritable. A doctor finally concluded that Christopher was suffering from too much stress.

These stories show small children facing big problems. Not all children are in tough shape. But a lot of them are—a lot more than we realize. And many don't know how to cope or express themselves. They need more than just a babysitting service. They need ministry that will help them grow up in a tough world. And to minister effectively, we need to be aware of the issues these kids are dealing with.

Complex Family Situations

Don't expect your children to live with a mom, a dad, a sibling and a dog. Children's families are as varied as the choices of vegetables and fruits at the supermarket. Some of the more common family situations:

● **Two-income families**—Fifty-one percent of mothers with children 1 year old or younger work outside the home. The proportion increases to 56 percent of moms who have children younger than 6 and then jumps to 73 percent of all moms who have kids 6 years old or older, reports the Bureau of Labor Statistics.[2]

Often kids from two-income families are neglected. Instead of showering kids with time and attention, the parents shower them with "things." If parents aren't careful, these kids can grow up to be materialistic—and even suicidal.

Life for kids who live in commuter marriages gets even more complicated. One 2-year-old who lives with his dad during the week has been to the airport so many times to visit his mom, who works in another city, that he calls all the airplanes "Mommy."[3]

● **Cohabiting families**—More and more families live together outside marriage, and the kids—often from a previous marriage— live with them. Today 2.6 million couples live together, a number that has almost doubled within the past 10 years, reports the U.S. Census Bureau.[4] "If recent trends continue," say University of Wisconsin, Madison, researchers who report living together is at a record high, "it will soon be the majority experience."[5]

Kids who live in such families sometimes have a hard time with commitment. They often don't understand the importance of marriage. They tend to have loose morals because of what they've witnessed at home.

● **Extended families**—Because of divorce, drug abuse, teenage pregnancy and financial hardship, more and more children are being raised by their grandparents instead of their parents. According to the U.S. Census Bureau, 3 million children live with grandpa and grandma. That's a 50 percent increase over the past 10 years.[6]

Extended families can be beneficial to children. But kids raised by grandparents or another family member may live in poverty since many older people live on limited incomes. These kids may also feel guilty and wonder what they did to cause their parents to leave them.

● **Single-parent families**—Today 15 million kids live in single-parent homes. And when asked how the number of children from single-parent families has changed within the past 10 years, 55 percent of teachers surveyed by the National Association of Elementary School Principals said it had greatly increased. And 40 percent more said the number of children from single-parent homes had increased somewhat.[7]

Part of the stress for children living in single-parent homes is dealing with limited financial resources. Although most divorce cases end up requiring a parent to pay child support, one out of four never does. Only half pay what the decree mandates.[8]

● **Stepfamilies**—Three out of four divorced people remarry, and 60 percent of them already have children. If current trends continue, your church may have more stepfamilies than traditional families by the year 2000.[9]

Adjusting to living in a stepfamily isn't easy for kids. According to researcher Dr. Patricia Papernow, it takes about seven years for a stepfamily to get used to living together.[10]

Whatever type of family children live with, it's important for kids to have close family ties. According to a University of California, San Francisco, study, sixth-graders who have strong family ties and have parents or guardians who encourage them to be independent are less likely to take risks such as fighting, drinking alcohol or having premarital sex.[11]

Stress

When Billy moved to a new town with his family, his parents assumed he would enter the gifted program at his new school. But Billy refused. When his parents asked him why, he said, "I don't need all that stress."

Many children today exhibit classic Type-A behavior. They're competitive, irritable, impatient and angry. This behavior leads to all kinds of stress symptoms. Kids get lots of headaches and stomachaches. Their palms sweat. Their hearts race. And they have trouble sleeping. One 8-year-old girl, who was stressed because her parents traveled so much, pulled her hair out in large clumps.

"I see 7-year-olds with schedules like young executives," says psychologist Paul Bracke, who studies Type-A behavior in children. Parents may push their children to fulfill their own unfulfilled dreams. Or busy parents push their kids to be as busy as they are.

Some parents may be unaware of their kids' stress. Child development expert T. Berry Brazelton says when parents wonder if their children are stressed, he says to them: "If you wonder if your lifestyle is affecting your kids, just look at yourself. If you're stressed, they are too."[12]

Accidents

Accidents are the leading cause of death for children over 9 months old. More children die by accident than all diseases combined, reports the Johns Hopkins Injury Prevention Center. Children under 1 year old are most vulnerable, and kids age 1 to 4 are the next most likely to die from accidents.

The most common types of accidental injuries that lead to death in children, according to the National Center for Health Statistics:

- Car accidents—37 percent
- Drowning—14 percent
- Fires—12 percent
- Homicide—10 percent
- Other (such as suffocation and choking on food)—27 percent

For children under 1 year old, suffocation and choking on food are major dangers. Preschoolers are three times more likely to drown than older children. And preschoolers are also about twice as likely as older children to get hurt by falling.

Yet adults are more fearful of child kidnapping than accidents. According to research by the Mayo Clinic in Rochester, Minnesota, almost three out of four mothers fear their children will be kidnapped by a stranger. Yet doctors estimate children have only a 1.5 in one million chance of ever being kidnapped.[13]

Drugs

Drug addiction can happen to a fifth-grader, a second-grader—even to a 2-day-old baby. In a survey of fifth- and sixth-graders by D.A.R.E. (Drug Abuse Resistance Education):

- One out of three expects to try alcohol by the time he or she gets to high school.
- One out of 10 knows where to buy drugs.
- One out of 10 has been offered wine or beer.
- One out of 33 has been offered marijuana.[14]

Although most kids have the option of saying no, babies aren't as lucky.

Children who experiment with drugs and alcohol start with

IN-DEPTH INFORMATION

The Boom in Drug-Infested Babies

As many as one out of six babies born each year may be exposed to illegal drugs before birth, says the journal Children Today.[15] Drug-exposed babies, especially babies exposed to crack, usually lack skills for initiative, free play, self-organization and follow-through. "These children are wired for 110 volts, living in a 220-volt world," says a Loveland, Colorado, volunteer coordinator for D.A.R.E., a non-profit organization that combats substance abuse.[16]

In Los Angeles, the number of babies that had been exposed to drugs entering the foster-care system jumped 453 percent within three years.[17]

—J.R.—

less obvious substances such as wine coolers or dangerous inhalants. Kids as young as 7 have been caught sniffing spray paint, model-airplane glue, typewriter correction fluid and nail polish remover.[18]

Children have also learned that they can get a "buzz" from medications such as Robitussin-CF or NyQuil, both of which have a high alcohol content. And one of the newer drugs kids abuse is a variation on Jell-O cubes, which they call slimeballs. Kids make innocent-looking Jell-O cubes with vodka.

To find out why children try alcohol, Weekly Reader asked fourth- to sixth-graders for their reasons. They said they drank alcohol:

● To fit in—39 percent
● To feel older—26 percent
● To have a good time—17 percent
● To not feel bad—9 percent
● For other reasons—7 percent
● No opinion—2 percent[19]

In addition to being concerned about children using alcohol and drugs, we also need to be concerned about taking care of children who decide not to use these substances. In New York, 12-year-old David Aupont almost died from being severely beaten and burned after he refused to smoke crack cocaine.[20]

IN-DEPTH INFORMATION

Drugs and Alcohol—Churches Mum on the Subject

The place where fourth- to sixth-graders say they learn the least about the dangers of drugs and alcohol is the church, reports a Weekly Reader survey. Where kids do learn about the dangers:
- School—52 percent
- Family—27 percent
- Television and the movies—14 percent
- Other kids—3 percent
- Nowhere—2 percent
- Church—1 percent[21]

—J.R.—

Abuse

About 1.5 million cases of child abuse and neglect are reported each year, according to the U.S. Department of Health and Human Services. The National Committee for the Prevention of Child Abuse identifies 2.4 million reported cases of child abuse and neglect. But most child abuse experts say those numbers are low. Other experts point out that these numbers are *reported* cases. Who knows how many children are actually abused without that abuse being reported?[22]

However many children are abused each year, the number is staggering. Experts say there are four general ways kids are abused.
- Physical abuse
- Sexual abuse (50 percent of the cases are incest)
- Emotional abuse
- Neglect (the most common of the four)

Though neglect is common it's difficult to detect. Neglected children don't get bruises or show any physical appearances of abuse. Neglect is the failure of a parent to take care of a child's basic needs: feeding the child; taking the child to the doctor when ill; keeping the child clean; making sure the child is safe; and making sure the child is in school. The Family Violence Research Program at the University of Rhode Island estimates that 2 to 6 million children are neglected every year.

Abuse takes its toll on children. According to research from the State University of New York at Albany, neglected and abused children tend to have lower intelligence and are more prone to depression and drug and alcohol problems.[23] Abused children often grow up to become criminals. In one study, 12 of 15 death row inmates admitted they'd been abused as children. A Denver study of 100 juvenile offenders revealed that 84 had been abused when they were kids.[24]

Poverty

We think of poor kids in the inner city or poor kids in Appalachia. But you may have poor children in your ministry and not even know it.

Dorchester Temple Baptist Church in Boston discovered this reality. Since the church's vacation Bible school included breakfast and lunch, one VBS worker noticed some children gobbled down their food as if they were starving. Investigating her observation, she discovered that, in fact, some kids actually were starving. The church then started serving breakfast at church school so kids could count on getting at least one meal a day.[25]

The number of children living in poverty in the United States is staggering. The House Select Committee on Children, Youth and Families found that:

● One of every five children in the United States is poor.
● One of every two black children lives in poverty.
● One of every four preschoolers is poor.
● Black and Hispanic children are two to three times more likely to live in poverty as white children.[26]

Poor children not only lack food, clothing and shelter, they often lack medical care. Preventable diseases, such as whooping cough, tetanus, measles, diphtheria, polio and tuberculosis kill millions of children every year. Even more children die from dehydration.[27]

Furthermore, the number of children living in poverty is rising. According to KIDS COUNT, a project of the Center for the Study of Social Policy in Washington, D.C., the number of kids living in poverty rose from 16 percent in 1979 to 20 percent today. The study also revealed that the child poverty rate rose in 41 states and the District of Columbia during the same time. In 1990, one out of every 16 U.S. families was living on welfare, and the American Public Welfare Association said that was the highest number it had ever seen.[28]

Homelessness

More than one-third of the nation's homeless are families with children. According to the United States Conference of Mayors, families with children make up more than half of some cities' homeless. For example:

- Norfolk, Virginia—81 percent
- Trenton, New Jersey—77 percent
- Chicago, Illinois—61 percent
- New York City—58 percent
- Kansas City, Kansas—55 percent[29]

Dr. Ellen Bassuk, one of the leading authorities on homeless families, estimates that about 750,000 children are homeless in the United States, and that half of those kids are younger than 5.[30]

Homeless children aren't in good shape. Many are literally starving, and many have health problems. "These children live under the most extreme conditions of adversity of any child population in the developed world," Dr. Irwin Redlener of New York Hospital told an Associated Press reporter. "They're the closest thing we have to refugees in the Third World." Redlener treats 200 homeless children a week from two medical vans. One of every two homeless children he sees needs immunizations. Many have asthma and ear infections.[31]

Ministering to Children's Needs

Ministering to children can happen only when we thoroughly understand children's interests and the issues they face. But knowing these issues can open doors to effective, innovative ministries. Consider how some churches have responded to these tough issues:

● Recognizing the drug problem among children in its community, Union Temple Baptist Church in Washington, D.C., offers a support program for kids as young as 11 who've been through drug rehabilitation.

● In Indianapolis, the Oasis of Hope church offers a program for first- to sixth-graders. Every day after school, kids come to the church for help with their school work. Since so many of the kids live on welfare, teaching children life skills can be vital to their developing the skills they need to pull out of the cycle of poverty.

● Because Glide Memorial United Methodist Church in San Francisco saw kids dealing with so many tough issues—such as homelessness, abuse, drugs and poverty—the church had the children write a book about their experiences. The result, *I Have Something to Say About This Big Trouble*, raises money for the church's children's ministry.

These—and dozens of other stories like them—illustrate how churches can and do meet the challenge of helping children in today's tough world. The remaining chapters of this book give specific ideas for how your church can meet the needs of your community's children.

Notes
■ ■ ■ ■

[1]David Elkind, *The Hurried Child*, (Reading, MA: Addison-Wesley, 1981), 3.

[2]Nina Darnton, "Mommy Vs. Mommy," Newsweek (June 4, 1990), 66.

[3]John Leo, "Marital Tales of Two Cities," Time (January 25, 1982), 83.

[4]"2.6 Million U.S. Couples Living Together: Census," Jet (February 4, 1991), 54.

[5]"Living Together Is at Record High: Study Says," Jet (May 16, 1988), 32.

[6]Jill Smolowe, "To Grandma's House We Go," Time (November 5, 1990), 86.

[7]"NAESP Principals' Opinion Survey: Meeting the Needs of Children in Single-Parent Families," National Association of Elementary School Principals press release (April 14, 1989).

[8]Thomas Mazario, "When Your Ex Won't Pay," Parents (March 1991), 63.

[9]"When Two Families 'Marry,' " Self (May 1989), 206.

[10]Margaret Jaworski, "Blended Is Splended?" Family Circle (January 8, 1991), 7.

[11]"Family Ties Make Teens Strong," Working Mother (November 1990), 134.

[12]Robert E. Hales, M.D., "Babes in Stressland," American Health (October 1989), 46-52.

[13]Various articles, Hotline (Winter 1990-1991), 1-5.

[14]"Kids & Drugs," USA Today (October 23, 1990).

[15]Barb Malone, "Cocaine Kids," CHILDREN'S MINISTRY Magazine (May/June 1991), 6-7.

[16]Traci McGraw, "Schools Face First Wave of Crack Babies," Loveland Daily Reporter Herald (February 4, 1991).

[17]Nancy Gibbs, "Shameful Bequests to the Next Generation," Time (October 8, 1990), 46.

[18]Paula Szegda, "The 'Children's Drug': Inhalants," Fridley Parents Communication Network (Spring 1990), 4.

[19]"What Kids Said About Drugs and Alcohol," Weekly Reader (February 22, 1991).

[20]"Reagan, Dinkins Send Wishes to N.Y. Boy, 12, Set Afire for Not Smoking Crack," Jet (March 26, 1990), 55.

[21]"What Kids Said About Drugs and Alcohol," Weekly Reader (February 22, 1991).

[22]Anthony Brandt, "Permanent Damage," Parenting (November 1990), 76-81, 198-200.

[23]"Abuse Takes Toll," USA Today (February 18, 1991).

[24]Brandt, "Permanent Damage," 78.

[25]Daniel Buttry, *Bringing Your Church Back to Life: Beyond Survival Mentality* (Valley Forge, PA: Judson, 1988), 81-82.

[26]"20% of U.S. Children Live in Poverty," Denver Post (October 2, 1989).

[27]Jeff Sellers, "Suffer the Children or Let the Children Suffer?" World Vision (February/March 1991), 19.

[28]Dennis Kelly, "Kids' Well-Being Suffered in 1980s," USA Today (February 1, 1991).

[29]"No Place to Call Home," Weekly Reader (February 8, 1991), 4-5, 8.

[30]Margaret Daly, "Homeless Families in America," Better Homes and Gardens (October 1988), 22.

[31]"Report: Kids Swell Ranks of Homeless," Loveland Daily Reporter Herald (September 20, 1988).

CHAPTER 3

LEADERSHIP THAT LASTS

■ ■ ■ ■ ■ ■ ■ ■ ■ ■ ■ ■ ■ ■ ■

BY JUDY WORTLEY

Quality leadership is a key to successful children's ministry. Your volunteers are your arms to hug children and your lips to tell them about Jesus' love. They make up the important team that makes your ministry effective.

Yet a recent survey of over 100 children's pastors and children's ministry directors asked, "What is your greatest need or the greatest problem you face at this time in your ministry?" Sixty-two percent said, "Recruiting leaders."

Your philosophy of recruitment and teacher training will influence the amount of time you give to these tasks. Understanding that recruitment and training go hand in hand will ease the load of simply getting people "recruited."

We often think if we find the "right" people, we could cut down our recruiting efforts. But unless we train adequately, even the "right" people can become frustrated and leave. Only as we train our leaders and watch their enthusiasm for their ministry grow will we see less turnover and more effective leadership.

Characteristics of a Good Volunteer

One day at church, a man—I'll call him Sam—said he knew I needed help in the children's ministry. He explained he had never worked with kids and didn't know if he could. Sam said, "I'm scared, but I'd like to give it a try." After talking with him and finding out about his background, we placed him in a classroom with a veteran Sunday school teacher.

Sam was so frightened the first month I was sure he'd quit. But he came to teacher training meetings, and I encouraged him over the telephone. When he had questions, he called me or the other teachers.

One year later Sam came to me in tears. He explained he had just received a wonderful gift. One of his students came in early before Sunday school and said: "Mommy this is the man! This is my favorite Sunday school teacher!"

Sam taught for the next seven years. I'd never have picked him out of a lineup of Sunday school teachers. In fact, he would have been the least likely candidate for the job, since he didn't have any experience.

Don't just look for the stereotypical children's workers. God has gifted many different people, and the gift of teaching is a great gift. Instead of focusing on a person's experience or skills in working with children, we should look for people who:

● have a teachable spirit. Some people are open for God to use them no matter where he places them.

● show flexibility. In ministering to children, flexibility is the key to sanity!

● have the desire to be a team player.

● are dependable. Look for people who do what they say.

● exhibit enthusiasm!

The Basics of Recruitment

Of course, finding the right people is only the beginning. You must also convince them to commit to working with children. You can enhance and build your recruitment skills in many ways. Let's look at some of the basics:

● **Define your areas of need.** Ask yourself: How many people do I need for Sunday school, children's church, mid-week programs, children's choir and special children's ministry events? You may discover you don't need as many people as you thought.

IN-DEPTH INFORMATION

Searching for Volunteers

Try one of these six methods to recruit volunteers. Select one that's best for you. Or combine a couple of methods and adapt them for your particular situation.

1. Public-appeal method—Advertise in Sunday morning church bulletins or weekly church newsletters. Announce children's ministry needs in adult Sunday school classes and from the pulpit.

Make it clear that interested people will get more information about children's ministry. And all of them won't become volunteers.

2. Telephone method—Recruit volunteers by calling church members. A phone call adds a more personal touch than the public-appeal method. Make the person feel comfortable over the telephone. And don't call during evening meals.

3. Volunteer-recruiters method—Have volunteers speak to prospective volunteers about working with children. They can answer every question a potential volunteer has because they have been there.

4. Come-and-find-out method—Many potential volunteers question whether children want them or how children interact with each other. Let potential volunteers observe children's classes. That way they will get to know the children before you ask them to decide. And they will have a better idea of what's expected.

5. Church-leadership method—Involve your senior minister. What a senior minister cares about, others will care about. Get names of potential volunteers from other leaders in the church, such as church board members and Sunday school teachers. And don't forget the church secretary.

When potential volunteers hear that the senior minister or a church leader recommends them as volunteer children's workers, their motivation to participate soars.

6. One-to-one method—Avoid appearing out of nowhere with a help request. Instead, build relationships first. Find out what the person enjoys doing. Then ask. Choose questions such as "Have you ever thought about teaching?" or "What do you think your ministry is going to be during the coming year?"

Match volunteers with their gifts. If Steve is a great organizer, use him behind the scenes.

—LES CHRISTIE—

● **Develop an accurate job description.** Volunteers want to know what you expect from them. Many people's reluctance to volunteer grows out of a bad experience in the past, when they might have felt thrown into a classroom with a teachers manual— then left for eternity!

Give volunteers information they'll need to begin teaching. I give teachers a packet of information that includes a letter of welcome, a personal information sheet to complete, a teacher/helper job description, and a covenant of commitment.

I also ask people to volunteer for one year. A full year greatly benefits the children. Kids need the same people ministering Jesus' love to them every week. A one-year commitment also gives a volunteer time to assimilate the purpose and philosophy of your ministry.

● **Pray.** As I began my ministry to children many years ago, I thought I was going to "help out a little" at church. Little did I realize how God would use me. The Lord gently guides us, leads us and meets our needs. Each new challenge gives us the opportunity to pray and see God answer.

● **Have teachers talk about their personal experiences.** During worship services, teachers could tell about blessings received from being with the children every week. These stories are encouraging, and they get others interested in joining the children's ministry team.

● **Keep the congregation informed.** Let people know the exciting things happening in your children's ministry. Publicizing your children's ministry creates interest in what you're doing. Use a variety of methods:

CREATIVE IDEA

Getting People Talking

Make buttons for your children's ministry volunteers to wear. You might make buttons saying "I'm needed!" "Ask me about my class!" or "I've got class!" People will ask, "What are the buttons for?" and your volunteers will have the opportunity to talk to them about becoming part of your children's ministry team.

—J.W.—

● Display projects made by the children on a bulletin board in the main traffic area of your church.

● Create colorful bulletin inserts to use a few times a year.

● Insert articles about children in your church newsletter.

● Have children do skits during worship.

How to Train Volunteers

Have you ever learned a new skill as an adult? How about learning to ride a bike, roller-skate or water-ski? It can be frightening and frustrating. And if we don't receive proper training, we usually walk away and declare, "Never again!"

Sadly, something similar happens in recruiting volunteers for children's ministry. Our volunteers don't receive adequate training, and they eventually conclude they can't do it. Without adequate training in the basics of working with children, the busy volunteer will be a short-term children's ministry leader.

Furthermore, your volunteers' skills will make a big difference in how secure the children will feel. A smooth-running, well-planned classroom gives children the security they need.

I believe teacher training has five purposes:

1. To impart your vision for children's ministry to your volunteers.

2. To build team spirit among all children's ministry volunteers.

3. To offer encouragement.

4. To provide needed social time for volunteers.

5. To equip volunteers with proper teaching techniques.

The most effective way to accomplish these purposes is through regular—even monthly—training workshops. You might begin with an introductory workshop during which you give an information packet to new teachers. This packet could include basic information, such as:

● how to take attendance,

● the time teachers should arrive for class,

● where supplies are kept,

● a curriculum sample,

● a yearly schedule of the subjects and dates of teacher training meetings and

● available audio visual equipment.

Then have classes that cover the basics of teaching. In these classes, teach volunteers about storytelling, discussions, discipline and how to plan a lesson. Require all volunteers to attend these classes. Children benefit when volunteers keep learning. A volunteer who's taught for many years will be a great encouragement to new volunteers.

Regular workshops also keep you in touch with volunteers. Ministering to children isn't a glitzy job. And though *you* know your volunteers are making a difference, *they* may not. So they need regular feedback from you, and these regular training sessions provide this opportunity.

Children's ministers often ask me, "How do you get your volunteers to come to the meetings?" There are two keys to persuading your volunteers to attend monthly meetings. First, convince them that these training sessions are as important as their Sunday morning classes. Second, make your meetings worthwhile. Who wants to go to a meeting that's boring and doesn't give participants greater confidence and skills for their ministry? Teacher training should be the highlight of your volunteers' month.

Leading Monthly Training Sessions

Before you jump in and do monthly teacher training, plan your meeting. You need to be well prepared. I plan one year in advance. In preparing to lead a session:

● List the supplies you'll need for the meeting. Will you need nametags, pens, scissors, decorations or visuals for the walls? Have a committee make and serve the refreshments. Don't ask your volunteers to bring refreshments; instead, use the workshops as an opportunity to make the volunteers feel special.

● About five days before the meeting, mail out a colorful, attractive note. Make it simple. Include the topics, time, place and room number. Use clip art. The appearance of the reminder should convey the message, "This will be a special meeting; don't miss it."

● As your volunteers arrive, greet them. Think of yourself as the host or hostess for this special event. Welcome volunteers warmly.

● Have volunteers sign in. Signing in gives volunteers a feeling of accountability. If you work with many volunteers, provide nametags so volunteers will be sure to know the names of people sitting around them. Make nametags to fit the time of year. Have pumpkin nametags in the fall and heart nametags in February.

● Set up the room differently for each meeting. Always set up fewer chairs than the number of volunteers you expect. A full room gives people the impression something exciting is about to happen. Psychologically it's better for people to pull up a chair than to walk into a room of 30 empty chairs.

● Decorate the room. Use crepe paper streamers and large visuals that reinforce the session's training topic. These decorations enhance the atmosphere of your meeting.

● Have coffee or iced tea ready for volunteers to pick up as they come into the room. Place a basket with bite-size candy bars near the coffee pot.

● Begin on time! Don't wait for stragglers. Volunteers who arrive late will soon learn they need to be punctual because the meeting will start without them.

● Plan the meeting with activities that will get the volunteer involved. Begin your meeting with an activity of some kind. This could be an activity that fits the topic for the evening or a game that will give volunteers a chance to relax and get acquainted. See chapter 6 for some game ideas or chapter 7 for craft ideas that will introduce the teachers to activities that work well with children.

● Encourage teachers to be creative. Have teachers make up a program, design a special project, write words to songs or make up skits. All these are ways to invite volunteers' creativity to spring forth.

● Choose training topics your teachers need most. Ask teachers what they'd like to learn. And don't think you need to have all the answers and do all the teaching. Have volunteers help teach. For example, teachers could present two skits: a humorous one on how to discipline incorrectly and then a skit that shows the proper way to discipline. Bring in guest speakers occasionally, or use a film.

● Give prizes to classes or age groups that have all their teachers and helpers attending the meeting. Make prizes fun. For example, give away hot fudge sundae gift certificates.

● The morning after the meeting, mail postcards to those who missed the meeting. Let these teachers know you missed them. But most of all, emphasize how they missed a great meeting!

Working With Volunteers

In working with volunteers, take on the attitude of a servant. When you do this, you will reap rich rewards. Since one goal in working with volunteers is to make them successful, being a servant is vital.

Being a servant isn't always easy, however. Sometimes a volunteer doesn't want to be part of the team. You may see a volunteer who lacks patience with children or is unwilling to attend training meetings. A volunteer may face personal problems at home, illness or stress.

It can be difficult to "fire" a volunteer, but for the children's sake, it may be necessary. If you feel you must fire a volunteer, do it with gentleness and love. Face this dilemma with prayer, love and discernment. God may be calling this volunteer to another area of ministry.

You *will* face problems with your volunteers. Where there are people, there will always be difficulties. A volunteer who calls you on Saturday night from another city saying he forgot to get a substitute is a problem. So are teachers who have difficulty working together. And so is the teacher who refuses to use the curriculum.

Your difficulties with volunteers may be as many as the volunteers you have. But in dealing with each of these volunteers, give each one the prayer and consideration the Lord has given you. Every situation is unique, so treat each one with care.

The pulse of your children's ministry comes from the hearts of your volunteers! Love them, challenge them, be their servant, and be their leader! Encourage them to look to the future to see the changed life of that one boy or girl. Show them how their hugs and smiles can wrap around the hearts of the children and hold them forever in God's love!

CHAPTER 4

GETTING PARENTS ON BOARD

■ ■ ■ ■ ■ ■ ■ ■ ■ ■ ■ ■ ■ ■ ■ ■

BY PAUL E. WHITE, PH.D.

O ne of the most challenging aspects of working with children is walking the tightrope of involving parents. On one hand, parental involvement is critical so that parents will know what you're doing and can reinforce your teachings at home. On the other hand, many parents resent involvement because they want *you* to teach their children.

Importance of Parental Involvement

Without parental support and involvement, ministering to children can be difficult, if not impossible. From both a biblical and practical perspective, parental involvement is vital.

When examining scripture, it's clear that *parents* are to spiritually train their children. Deuteronomy 6:6-7 says: "These commandments that I give you today are to be upon your hearts. Impress them on your children. Talk about them when you sit at home and when you walk along the road, when you lie down and when you get up."

Throughout Proverbs, children are encouraged to pay attention to the instruction of their parents (Proverbs 1:8-9). And many proverbs were written by a father to his children (see Proverbs 2:1 and 3:1). Probably the most familiar Bible verse about parents' involvement is Proverbs 22:6: "Train a child in the way he should go, and when he is old he will not turn from it."

The responsibility of parental training is re-emphasized in Ephesians 6:4: "Fathers, do not exasperate your children; instead, bring them up in the training and instruction of the Lord."

So the Bible is clear: Parents need to be involved in spiritually training their children.

From a practical perspective, church workers have only a limited impact on children. We're with them only one to two hours a week. Who spends the most time with children? The parents. Parents have more influence than anyone else on their children's faith. Yet many parents aren't giving their children the spiritual food they need.[1]

Unfortunately, typical approaches to getting parents more involved don't work. Most of us want to solve the problem as quickly and directly as possible. So when we decide parents aren't as involved as they should be, we set out to change the situation— usually by telling the parents they should be more involved.

The result? If we're lucky, nothing happens. But too often the result is a strained relationship between the children's workers and the parent.

Since this approach doesn't help the situation, we go to plan B: We do nothing, say nothing and become steamed by parents' lack of involvement. What results? We develop bad attitudes toward the parents. And a less-than-healthy atmosphere for teaching children emerges.

Getting Parents Involved

But there's hope. You can involve parents in many ways. Your goal for parental involvement will vary depending on the children's ministry and each family's needs. Thus you must first determine how you want parents to be more involved. For example:

• You may want parents to bring their children to ministry

activities. This commitment might involve arranging car pools for some kids.

● You may want parents to become more aware of what's going on with their children spiritually. You could provide parenting workshops to help in this area. And you could include news about your ministry and the children in your church newsletter.

● You may want parents to volunteer their time by teaching Sunday school or leading in some other way. Chapter 3 addressed how to recruit and train volunteers—which could include parents.

● You may hope parents will take a more active role in spiritually educating their children at home. This goal might involve providing parenting classes as well as resources for parents to use at home.

After determining your goal, figure out *how* to get parents involved. In working with children and families in a variety of settings, I've found the first step is to try to understand the situation from the parents' perspective. Why do parents bring their children to Sunday school? What do they want for their children? What do they want for themselves as a result of their children's involvement?

Instead of judging parents, assume they have good intentions. Most want the best for their children, and are trying to do the best they can with the resources they have. Many parents feel short-changed on time and money.

Once you evaluate the parents' perspective, communicate your understanding of their situation. This allows you to confirm your observations and show parents that you understand their situation.

Communicate to parents your goals for their children. See if these goals are acceptable to them. Then ask parents for suggestions. Incorporate part of their suggestions into what you're doing with the children. This communicates that you value the parents' input.

This may sound time consuming, but you can do this simply and quickly. For example, when Mrs. Jones brings Johnny to a Sunday school class, have a dialogue something like this:

You: Hi, Johnny. How are you doing today?

Johnny: Fine.

You: That's great. Hi, Mrs. Jones. I'm glad to see you again. Thanks for bringing Johnny to class. Hey, I understand your Sunday school class is studying Romans. I'm glad you can do that while Johnny is here.

IN-DEPTH INFORMATION

Parents' Experiences When They Were Children

Many parents' expectations of helping their children grow spiritually stem from what they experienced—or didn't experience—when they were children. Thinking back to when they were 5 to 12 years old, the percentage of parents who remembered:

	30- to 39-year-olds	40- to 49-year-olds
Talking with their mother about faith	17%	17%
Talking with their father about faith	12%	10%
Having family devotions	18%	10%
Doing family projects to help other people	11%	14%
Attending Christian education classes and events[2]	83%	70%

—J.R.—

Mrs. Jones: It's an interesting class for me.

You: By the way, you may not know this, but Johnny is learning about the Apostle Paul's missionary journeys right now. I'd appreciate any suggestions you might have for making class more interesting for him.

Mrs. Jones: I think you're doing a great job. But I do have one idea: What about sending home some Bible verses that relate to the lesson you're learning that we can read as a family during the week?

You: Super! I'll try that. Well, I'll try to talk to you more later. Have a good class!

Through this interaction, you can build an alliance with the parent and establish a sense of teamwork. And getting the parents' input—even though it may be minimal—may help some parents with guilt. Parents often fight an overwhelming sense of guilt. They feel guilty for not spending more time with their children. They feel guilty for working instead of being home full time. They feel guilty for not setting a good example.

When people feel guilty, they tend to avoid situations that make them feel even more guilty. If parents feel guilty when they talk to us, they'll avoid us. Therefore, the more we support and encourage parents, the less opportunity exists for parents to feel guilty in our relationship with them.

To build quality relationships with parents takes time—and creativity. When we see parents only in one context, the relationship can develop only to a certain level. But relationships flourish when we have multiple interactions. Watch for parents in the supermarket or at the local mall, and stop to talk. Arrange a lunch with them during the workday. If we talk to parents only when they drop off their kids at Sunday school, the relationship won't go far.

An Alternative: Family Sunday School

Instead of trying to get parents to participate in your existing Sunday school program, why not create a Sunday school for families? In this Sunday school class, we can teach parents how to spiritually train their children in a family setting.

Each week three or four families meet together with their children during Sunday school. One family, designated as the "lead" family, trains the other parents with the church's support and input. This family gives the biblical rationale for the parents'

CREATIVE IDEA

Building Relationships With Parents

Building relationships with parents does take time, but it doesn't need to take all your time. To build relationships with parents, try these ideas.

● Look for opportunities to chat with parents at church functions. Face-to-face interaction has the most impact. Find parents during coffee hours or potluck dinners.

● Write a note. During the week, drop a postcard or short letter to the parent. Writing each child's parents once every six months is reasonable. Communicate how much you appreciate having the child in your class.

● Call parents. And don't call them only when you want something. Just check in and ask how their children are doing. Then ask how *they're* doing.

● Visit parents at home. One church's children's minister does this on the child's birthday, by bringing a birthday balloon for the child. This creative way doesn't seem so imposing to some parents.

—P.W.—

teaching their children about faith.

This lead family then models how to teach children and includes the parents in the teaching process. *How* the teaching is done differs as much as the families themselves. Some families use standard Sunday school curricula while others primarily sing and pray together. Some families use Christian children's videos while others develop their own lessons and crafts.

I see a lot of benefits to this family-style Sunday school class. Parents—not Sunday school teachers—educate their children. Parents rather than the children are the primary focus of the training. Children learn in groups with children of a lot of different ages instead of kids of one age. And, best of all, families transfer what they learn at church to their home.

Providing Help for Parents

Parents, like everyone else, become discouraged and tired. A listening ear, empathetic response and a word of encouragement give many parents the boost they need.

Sometimes, however, parents look to the church for specific resources. Many times parents want to know of a good book that will help with a specific issue they're facing, such as kids who bite, a child who swears, sex education, family devotions or tips on handling a child who is becoming a teenager. Since so many books are on the market, they feel overwhelmed and don't know which to choose.

Therefore, refer parents to good books you've read. You could also recommend parent-training video series or parenting seminars. Preview the videos and get detailed information on the seminars so you'll know the perspective before you recommend them.

Ministering to Single-Parent Families

About one out of five families is led by a single parent.[3] Therefore, when ministering to parents, be sensitive to single parents.

Single parents have fewer resources available to cope with the daily demands of life. They usually have less time, money and physical and emotional energy than most two-parent families.

That's why most single parents feel overwhelmed. And they need your support.

One misconception about single-parent families is that "once a divorce is final, the conflict stops." But conflicts with the ex-spouse can continue for several months—even years. Parents who are no longer married may bicker over visitation, child-support payments, extended family members (especially grandparents) and stepfamily members.

Children of single-parent families struggle with a lot of issues. Children often blame themselves for the failure of the marriage and feel guilty. Children frequently feel a sense of grief over the loss of a parent. Finally, many children are angry. They're angry at their parents. They're angry at themselves. And they're angry at God.

What can we do to help these families?

● **Be understanding.** Don't condemn single parents and their children because of their circumstances. Too many churches add more guilt to the large amount of guilt single-parent families already feel.

● **Be flexible.** Know that some children won't be in Sunday school every Sunday because they're visiting the other parent. Instead of giving attendance awards to kids who attend every Sunday, think of other ways to affirm kids. For example:

● Give attendance awards to children who are in town and come to your church.

● Mail take-home papers to children who leave town to visit another parent so they'll feel like a part of the class.

● If the children leave town on the weekend, encourage them to attend a church in the other city. If possible, recommend a church you know. Then award kids who attend church when they're in the other city.

● **Be a resource.** Volunteer to babysit so the parent can have time alone. Invite the family over for dinner. You'll win their hearts and gain grateful friends!

A Parenting Ministry

This chapter has explained various ways to involve parents in your children's ministry. Unfortunately, many parents don't want to get involved—either because they themselves are not active Christians or they're ignorant of their responsibility to train their children spiritually. Some just lack the emotional resources to commit to this process.

But that doesn't mean we sit back and give up. We *can* get parents involved in spiritually educating their children. We just need to be creative. And trust that God will give us the wisdom to help parents grow in becoming active participants in their children's spiritual training.

Notes
■ ■ ■ ■

[1]Eugene C. Roehlkepartain, "Are You Stunting Your Teenager's Spiritual Growth?" PARENTS OF TEENAGERS Magazine (June/July 1990), 12-14.

[2]Peter L. Benson and Carolyn H. Eklin, *Effective Christian Education: A National Study of Protestant Congregations, a summary report on faith, loyalty, and congregational life* (Minneapolis: Search Institute, 1990), 48.

[3]*The Youth Ministry Resource Book*, edited by Eugene C. Roehlkepartain, (Loveland, CO: Group Publishing, 1988), 30.

Part Two:
Teaching Techniques

CHAPTER 5

LEARNING BY DOING

■ ■ ■ ■ ■ ■ ■ ■ ■ ■ ■ ■ ■ ■ ■ ■

BY TERRY VERMILLION

What I hear, I forget.
What I see, I remember.
What I do, I learn.
—Chinese proverb

All year, Jeremy yelled out answers during Sunday school. He constantly interrupted the class, and screamed at anyone who disagreed with him. One Sunday the class acted out a skit. In the skit Latanna, the mother, was to win an argument with her son Jeremy any way she could. She interrupted Jeremy. She screamed at him. And she threatened him.

In the discussion that followed Jeremy yelled, "That's just the way my mother talks to me. She interrupts me. And if I don't agree with her, she yells." That day, the kids learned something important about Jeremy.

What Is Active Learning?

Active learning means children learn by doing. When a Sunday school class builds a tower out of Popsicle sticks then discusses how cooperating helped them build it, that's active learning. When children race on their stomachs toward a goal then talk about the lame man who tried to get into the healing pool, that's active learning. When a preschooler tastes pomegranates and decides they taste a little like strawberries, that's active learning.

Active learning is fun and builds relationships. It involves everyone. And it involves interaction among children.

But when the children sit in chairs and a leader tells a story, that's *not* active learning.

Instead of having the leader impart knowledge, active learning helps children make discoveries. The leader guides the activity but doesn't control what children learn. This makes active learning risky for the leader; you can't predict the outcome.

For example, you may feel the children need a lesson in cooperation. But in active learning, some children may learn not to always depend on others. When children build a Popsicle-stick tower, you assume that children will learn cooperation is good. But if the tower falls three times, some children may decide that, although cooperation is fun, one child can build the tower better than the group.

The leader needs to accept the discoveries of the group as the workings of the Holy Spirit. Sometimes the leader learns more than the children. In this example, the children might learn that it can sometimes be hard to work together, so we have to keep trying to be successful.

Children Learn in Different Ways

James was the choir director's favorite, although the director tried to treat all the children equally. Still, James learned the words to the songs so fast—even though he wasn't reading yet. If he heard a song once he could hum the tune. He always hung around after choir to ask questions about the piano, or about music. He always left singing.

Then James' parents told the choir director James would have to quit the choir. James was doing so poorly in first grade that he had to spend more time on his homework. The choir director was crushed. How could a little boy that seemed so bright be such a poor student?

In *Frames of Mind*, Howard Gardner defines intelligence as "… the ability to solve problems, or to create products, that are valued within one or more cultural settings."[1] James could recognize and reproduce a series of notes, remember a pattern of tones over a long period of time, memorize words to a song and copy rhythm patterns. James was intelligent, but his intelligence wasn't developed in the areas tested by his school.

Through work with brain-damaged patients and healthy preschoolers Gardner theorized that there are at least seven different types of intelligence. We each possess all seven, but one or more is stronger than the others in each of us. The type of intelligence that's stronger makes a difference in the way we learn, the interests we have and the way we live. The "7 Learning Styles" box on page 58 explains Gardner's seven types of learners.

The basic school curriculum of reading, writing and arithmetic deals most prominently with linguistic and logical intelligence. The church combination of sermons, readings and hymns deals entirely with the linguistic and musical intelligences. Therefore the church doesn't easily reach God's people who learn in other ways.

Through active learning we can claim the rest of God's people. For example, see how the following activity, called Small Change, works.

In this activity students sit in a circle on the floor with their legs crossed. Everyone says the following chant and does the motions indicated.

Oh now, oh now (pat floor twice with both hands)
Ugh ugh (clap hands twice)
Chickadee, chickadee (wave right hand, wave left hand)
Ugh (clap hands once)

The group repeats the chant several times to set up a rhythm. When everyone is chanting and clapping together, the leader starts a motion that can be done with two hands such as patting the ears. The leader does this throughout one verse of the chants.

On the second verse, the child to the right of the leader does

IN-DEPTH INFORMATION

7 Learning Styles

In his book *Frames of Mind*, Howard Gardner identifies the following seven types of learners, what they like and how they learn best.[2]

Type of Learners	What They Like	How They Learn Best
1. Linguistic	Reading, writing and telling stories	Through the written and spoken word
2. Logical/ mathematical	Experimenting, working with patterns and math	Through reasoning and problem-solving
3. Spatial	Drawing, building and working with things such as machines	Through visualizing and creating things
4. Musical	Singing, playing an instrument and listening to music	Through pitch, rhythm and timbre
5. Kinesthetic	Doing physical activities such as dance, sports and crafts	Through comparing intended action with actual results
6. Interpersonal	Leading, building friendships, working in groups and talking	Through interaction with others
7. Intrapersonal	Meditating, reflecting and feeling	Through working alone

—T.V.—

an action. That child must use one hand exactly as the leader did and change the action of the other hand. For example, the child would pat one ear and then maybe pat one eye.

On the third verse the third person must use one hand exactly as the second child did and change one. This continues until the action returns to the leader.

After the activity, ask children to close their eyes and think about how the action changed from person to person. When they open their eyes ask if the hand action at the end was different from the first. Ask how this happened.

Then ask: If you make a small change in the way you act, how does it affect others? What would happen if you smiled more? Gently lead the children into discovering how a little change in their actions can change everyone else's actions.

As you do this, don't force your ideas on the children. Let them explore the learning in their own way. At the end ask them to think of one small change they could make that would make this group more like Jesus would want it to be. Then have children each name one change they'll make.

This activity involved all seven of our different learners. The linguistic child loved the sound of the nonsense words. The logical-mathematical child liked the repeating pattern and approached the selection of an action as a problem to solve. The musical child locked into the rhythm and the pitch of the chant. The spatial learner enjoyed visualizing different hand movements to choose from. The kinesthetic child picked up the pattern of the hand movements. The interpersonal child watched how others reacted to the game and chose an action to amuse, surprise or move the game along. The intrapersonal child chose an easy action and reflected on the experience during the quiet time.

Wow! With one activity, you reached a lot of different learners. How many children would you have reached if you had asked them to listen to you read a story?

Doing Active Learning

Active learning involves four parts: plan, action, reflection and application. Let's see the importance of each of these elements:

● **Plan**—Plan what goal you want to accomplish with the activity. For example, do you want children to learn the names of the Old Testament books? Or do you want children to learn to listen when others are talking? In planning the active-learning experience, remember the younger your children are, the more

WORKSHEET

Choosing an Active-Learning Activity

How do you evaluate whether an activity is good active learning?
Checkmark your answers to each of the following questions:

	Yes	No
Does the activity encourage everyone to participate?	☐	☐
Is the activity fun or interesting to the children?	☐	☐
Is the activity kind to everyone?	☐	☐
Is the activity age-appropriate?	☐	☐
Does the activity have a definite beginning and end?	☐	☐
Does the activity further the message you want to teach?	☐	☐
Is the activity suitable for your particular group of children?	☐	☐
Does the activity promote positive feelings?	☐	☐
Does the activity boost self-esteem?	☐	☐
Does the activity reflect an awareness of different cultures disabilities?	☐	☐
Does the activity avoid emphasizing physical attributes?	☐	☐
Does the activity avoid requiring a specific skill?	☐	☐

If you can answer yes to these questions, you have a great active-learning activity!

—T.V.—

simple and concrete your activities need to be.

● **Action**—Explain the activity enthusiastically so all the children want to participate. Get the children's attention by varying the pitch, speed and volume of your voice. For example, you might want to occasionally look furtively over your shoulder then whisper the directions. Or talk fast when introducing the activity and then give the directions slowly.

Take part in the activity. There are no spectators in active learning. Just let children decide how to do the activity after you've explained it. Resist the temptation to tell them how to do it right.

Stay tuned to the mood of the group. If the activity isn't working, stop. Some activities may not go the way you planned. If the activity is going well, keep your eye on the time. Activities are most effective if you quit while the children still want more.

● **Reflection**—At the end of the activity, create circles of five

EVERITT, YOU WERE SOOooooOOoo RIGHT IN OUR TEACHERS MEETING! THEY <u>DO</u> LEARN BETTER BY DOING.

or six children with one adult. Allow a brief period of quiet time for the children to reflect on the activity. You might ask a question or just tell them to think about the activity.

After the quiet time, ask questions to start the discussion. When working with preschoolers, recap the activity first, then ask questions. If children aren't making any connections, try some gentle leading. For example, say: I felt crowded when we stood on the book. How did it make you feel? Once children have identified what they've learned, move to the fourth part of active learning.

● **Application**—Give children a small task to incorporate their learning—to see the results of what they learned. For example, you might have children make a promise, pray, write what they learned or tell someone in the group what they learned.

After playing Small Change (the activity described on page 57), one girl said: "You know, there's been a spider web on that light fixture for weeks. I could get a broom and knock it down, but I never have."

A boy then said, "There's one over the window, too."

So the leader handed a broom to the girl who then knocked down her spider web. Then she gave the broom to the boy who cleaned the spider web from the window. He then passed the broom to another child who had found another spider web. I hadn't ever imagined that children would draw this conclusion from this activity, but it made sense. The children made a small change in the condition of their room.

Making the Bible Come Alive

A teacher on the island of Guam complained, "How can I teach Robert Frost's poem *Stopping by the Woods on a Snowy Evening* when no one in my class has ever seen snow, a woods, horses or a village?"

That's the challenge we have in teaching the Bible to children. Many children have never seen a well except for a wishing well at a shopping mall. Some children have never seen a fishing net or an olive tree. But the Bible mentions these things. So what can you do?

Provide opportunities for children to experience the things the

Bible talks about. Keep Arabic clothes on hand for kids to use as costumes during appropriate classes. For animals mentioned in the Bible, find stuffed animals and put them in the play area. Serve dates as a snack. Let children experience things the Bible mentions so the Bible isn't so foreign.

Active Learning in Children's Ministry

The thing that sets children's programs in the church apart from other children's activities is the spiritual emphasis. Children can talk to God, listen to God, praise God, thank God and petition God. Active learning in the church gives children a lot of ways to worship and learn about God.

How do you do active learning with children in the church? First, prepare. Then use active learning to help kids experience the scripture. Follow the activity with discussion and application. Here are three active-learning experiences for three different age groups. All are based on the same scripture.

● ● ●

Lesson: God provides
Best for: Preschoolers
Scripture: Matthew 6:26
Overview: Children will find food God provides for animals. Then they'll thank God for giving food to the animals.
Plan: Locate a safe area outdoors. Scatter acorns, sunflower seeds or other natural foods for animals where children can easily find them. Do this right before the lesson to keep birds from eating all the food before you're ready.
Action: Take children outside and tell them to look for food that animals eat. Some will find leaves or grass. Help those who can't find anything to discover the seeds.
Reflection: When everyone has something, gather the group into a circle. Tell children to look closely at the food they found. Have them think about the color. The smell. The texture. Have them tell which animal would like the food they picked up. Then read the scripture.
Application: Have children bow their heads and close their

eyes. Thank God for giving food to the animals. Pray: Dear God, thank you for giving this food to the animals. Amen.

Have the children each put their food in a place where they think an animal will find it.

• • •

Lesson: God provides
Best for: K-3
Scripture: Matthew 6:25-27
Overview: Children search for animal food and thank God for giving food to the animals.
Plan: Locate a safe area outdoors. Make pictures of animal foods found in this area. Then, depending on the number of children you have, make a piece of paper with three to four pictured items for every four children. On one piece of paper you might have a leaf, a blade of grass, a flower and an acorn. On another sheet of paper you may have a nut, seeds, a pine cone and pine needles.
Action: Form groups of four. Give each group a paper with the pictured items to find. Tell children not to pick up the items but remember where they saw them so they can show others. Give children time to find the things then call the group back together.

Then have the whole group visit the things one of the groups of four found. After all the items have been found, go to the next small group until all the small groups have shown where their items are.
Reflection: Gather in a circle. Ask children to name as many foods as they can remember. Ask which animals God is feeding in this area. Ask how the animals find the food. Read the scripture.
Application: Pray, thanking God for providing food for the animals and for us.

• • •

Lesson: God provides
Best for: Grades 4-6
Scripture: Matthew 6:25-34
Plan: Get a picnic basket. Get an individually packaged drink and an individually wrapped snack for each child. Hide the snacks and drinks outside. Hang the snacks and drinks from tree

branches. Hide snacks in the grass. Have an adult guard the area to keep birds and other animals away.

Action: Hold up the picnic basket and tell the children that you've decided to take them on a picnic. Lead the group to a spot near the hidden food where kids can't see the food. Have the group sit around the picnic basket.

Read the scripture. Ask children to guess what's in the picnic basket. Then ask one child to look in the basket and tell the group what's inside. When the child tells the group the picnic basket is empty, act disappointed. Ask if anyone remembers what the scripture said about finding food.

Then have children look for food outside. Let them find and recover the food. Then gather everyone together to eat.

Reflection: While eating ask if children worried that they wouldn't get a snack. Ask if they expected to find snacks where they did. Have children close their eyes as you reread verses 31-34 aloud. With their eyes still closed, ask the children to silently think of five things they've worried about that they blew out of proportion. Then have children open their eyes and stand.

Application: Form a circle with everyone holding hands. Ask children in the circle to each name something they won't worry about this week. Close with prayer asking God to help us not to worry about things that aren't very important.

Notes
■ ■ ■ ■

[1]Howard Gardner, *Frames of Mind: The Theory of Multiple Intelligence* (New York: Basic Books, 1983), X.

[2]Kathy Faggella and Janet Horowitz, "Different Child, Different Style," Instructor (September 1990), 49-54.

CHAPTER 6

GREAT GAMES FOR KIDS

■ ■ ■ ■ ■ ■ ■ ■ ■ ■ ■ ■ ■ ■ ■

BY TERRY VERMILLION

G ames may be the most versatile part of children's ministry.
They can be part of an active-learning experience. They can
be crowdbreakers or community-builders. They may help kids
burn energy or give them a new experience. Or you may play
games just to give kids some fun.

Sometimes it's hard to define what's a game and what's not. For
example, I do an activity called Mime Circles with my elementary
kids. In this activity, each child gets a partner and forms a double
circle with partners facing each other. The leader calls out a topic
such as "something you do in the morning," "something to eat" or
"a form of transportation." The partner on the inside circle acts out
the topic. The partner on the outside circle tries to guess what the
action is. If the outside person guesses correctly, children trade
places. Children on the inside circle then move one person to the
right, and we repeat the activity.

Is this a game or a drama improvisation? You can make this
activity into an active-learning experience if you add a time for
reflection and application (see chapter 5).

What makes a game work well with children?

● First, a good game has a clear goal, such as getting over the line, guessing the action or catching a ball.

● Next, a game has clear rules. All children know what they're expected to do and when to do it.

● A game must call for a skill or a motivation that keeps children interested in finding out how it will end.

● Finally, a game gives everyone a sense of involvement.

Competitive and Non-Competitive Play

Competition, with its emphasis on winning and losing, builds team spirit, develops skills and sharpens both mind and body. Competition isn't bad; it's what children do with competition that can be bad. It can lead to name-calling, feelings of inferiority and bullying.

In working with children at church, we need to ask ourselves: Does competition teach what the church teaches? Is beating the other team what we want to teach? Do we want children to feel like winners and losers?

I believe non-competitive games are better for children because they promote self-confidence and self-esteem. Non-competitive games are kind. They promote group-building. They involve cooperation. And they allow everyone to participate, not just those who have a special skill. In most cases, non-competitive games fit better with the church mission.

Terry Orlick, an author who believes in the importance of non-competitive games, has published two books of cooperative games. The back cover of his book *The Second Cooperative Sports & Games Book* explains his philosophy: "Terry Orlick's approach to sports is simple: when people play together and not against each other, everyone has more fun." [1]

Competitive kids will often resist non-competitive play. They'll try to add competition to the game. Or they'll complain that since no one wins, the game doesn't have a point.

To change this, start by introducing familiar non-competitive games. Tag is a good game to start with. Keep the play area small by setting boundaries so that running skill doesn't become a factor.

You can also play competitive games, but change the rules so winning isn't important. For example, play non-competitive softball. When the batter doesn't hit the ball after three tries, the batter becomes the first baseman. The first baseman moves to second base and so on. The right fielder runs in to join the batting lineup.

In addition to playing competitive games that you altered, try non-competitive games that are included in books such as Terry Orlick's *Cooperative Sports & Games Book*[2] and *The Second Cooperative Sports & Games Book*. Also, books such as *Playfair*,[3] *New Games Book*,[4] *More New Games & Playful Ideas*[5] and *New Games for the Whole Family*[6] contain a lot of non-competitive games.

CREATIVE IDEA

Dealing With Competition

At times, your children may have to play competitive games. For example, your children's ministry group may visit another church group that has planned an entire program of competitive games. Or your church may ask you to coach the church basketball team.

If this happens, set a few simple rules. Don't let children call other children—or themselves—names. This includes times when children make mistakes during the game and call themselves "dummies."

Explain that God loves every child on both teams. Have children find something they like about the other team and tell the players. Have children cheer a good performance no matter which team did it. Have children learn—and act—on this rule: Winning *isn't* the only thing; loving each other *is*.

—T.V.—

Choosing Games

If you're planning a series of games or a Saturday game day, vary the activity level of the games. Start with a moderately active game then move to a highly active game. Do a quiet game next. Then finish with active games. Use this game progression:

• First have children play non-threatening, whole-group games. The least threatening games for children include the whole group, are controlled by one leader and don't require touching. These games let children move around a lot in a short period of time. Good examples of these types of games are included in *Fun Group Games for Children's Ministry.*[7]

● Then play games for small groups. These games help children recognize faces without requiring them to get too close to other children. A good example of this is Musical Instruments, in *Fun Group Games for Children's Ministry.*[8]

Form teams of two to 10 players. Have each group move into its own space (different rooms, if possible) and—without any props or materials—create a musical instrument complete with sound and movement. Give groups exactly five minutes. Then have groups each perform their instrument. Re-form different groups and play again.

● Finally, do games that involve interaction with one person, such as the Mime Circles described at the beginning of this chapter. At this point you can introduce games with appropriate touching. Even upper-elementary-age children will hold hands at this point. But if you played a game that required fifth-graders to hold hands at the beginning of a game time, most kids wouldn't do it.

Games for Young Children

Children usually don't play with other children until halfway through their third year. Until then, most children play alongside of each other, playing their own games. Sometimes you see 2-year-olds pass toys back and forth and copy each other's actions, but they're not really playing together.

Many 2-year-olds will play a one-to-one game such as Pat-a-Cake with an adult. But most 2-year-olds will refuse to play the same game with another 2-year-old. For this age group, games for children to play "alone with the group" are best.

For example, do singing games where each child does hand motions to a song. Or make up games where you give simple directions to the children and have them mimic your actions. For example, ask: Who can touch a finger to a knee? Who can stomp their feet? Who can jump up and down? Who can sit down?

Try this game with 2- and 3-year-olds: Together sing the words "God loves me and God loves you" to the tune of "Twinkle,

Twinkle, Little Star," singing the same phrase six times. When you sing the word "God" point to the ceiling, and encourage the children to also point to the ceiling. When you sing the word "me" point to yourself. When you sing the word "you" point to someone else. If the toddlers want to keep playing, substitute the names of children in the group for the words "me" and "you." For example, sing "God loves Kelly and God loves Lee" and point to those people as you sing. Make sure you use everyone's name.

This game is a community-builder. How? Most community-builders involve working together as a group to accomplish a purpose. This game works as a community-builder because it gives 2-year-olds a common experience. Children see each other and the leader as non-threatening. (They see that the leader isn't going to grab their hands and make them do something.) They develop a relationship with the leader. And when you use their names in the song, it helps them learn the other children's names while building their self-esteem when they hear their own names sung.

Four- and 5-year-olds are more capable of group games. The developmental chart in the appendix on pages 216 and 217 explains some of the social aspects of this age group.

A game I like to play with preschoolers is called Touching Together. This game encourages preschoolers to share an object and work together to accomplish a goal. It also offers a non-threatening way for 4- and 5-year-olds to be close and touch each other.

Before children arrive, assemble five or more objects of increasing size. For example, you might choose a pencil for the first item, a block for the second item, a book for the third item, a large-format magazine (such as LIFE) for the fourth item and a carpet square as the last item.

When you're ready to play, lay the pencil on the floor. Then ask: How many of you can put one finger on the pencil at one time? The children will giggle as they all try to wiggle together to touch the pencil.

Then ask: How many of you can put two fingers on the pencil? How many can put a nose on the pencil?

Then remove the pencil and put down the block. Ask: How many of you can put one finger on the block? one elbow? one knee?

With the book, ask: How many of you can put one finger on the book? one heel? one ear?

Continue with the rest of the objects and suggest larger body parts. Finish by asking: How many people can stand on the carpet square?

IN-DEPTH INFORMATION

Choosing Games for Different Ages

Not sure which games work best with which ages? These types of games work with these age groups.

2- and 3-year-olds
Games can involve jumping, crawling, walking, and hand motions as long as the game doesn't depend on precise movement. Look for games that are simple to explain and can be demonstrated during the game. Games where everyone performs alone are best. For example, Simon Says works well with this age group.

4- and 5-year-olds
Games can include running to and from a point, hopping, jumping forward and backward or throwing and catching a large ball. Children will work with a partner. "Pretending" games, such as "Can you pretend to be a cat?" are good choices.

6- to 8-year-olds
Play games that have a variety of small and large movements. Directions can include five or six activities at one time. At this age, children think games with rhymes and chants are fun. A good example is the Small Change game on page 57 of chapter 5.

9- to 12-year-olds
Games can be physically active with complicated rules. Play games that have teams or small groups. Look for games that have an obvious ending. For example, Tag doesn't have an obvious ending. Children could play it for hours and never know when to stop—except when they got tired of playing it.

—T.V.—

Games for Elementary-Age Children

When working with older children, you can play more complicated games. Older children can move and use their bodies in a variety of ways such as hopping, running, skipping and jumping. Upper-elementary-age children can play games that require fine motor control such as spelling words out of alphabet macaroni.

Try the following game, Loose Noose, with 9- to 12-year-olds.

In this game, you'll need three to six sponge balls for each group playing. Set up a folding chair about 20 feet from the starting line.

Form a circle with four or five children holding hands. Put three sponge balls in the center of the group. The group must move all three balls from the starting line, around the folding chair 20 feet away and back to the starting line without letting go of hands. If the group loses a ball, the entire circle, while holding hands, must get it. Time the group to see if it can improve its own time.

Then give the kids six balls. Can they match their previous time when they played the game with three balls? Focus each group's attention on improving its own score, not doing the activity faster than other groups.

Notes
■ ■ ■ ■

[1]Terry Orlick, *The Second Cooperative Sports & Games Book* (New York: Random House, 1982).

[2]Terry Orlick, *Cooperative Sports & Games Book* (New York: Pantheon, 1978).

[3]Matt Weinstein and Joel Goodman, *Playfair: Everybody's Guide to Noncompetitve Play* (San Luis Obispo, CA: Impact, 1980).

[4]*New Games Book*, edited by Andrew Fluegelman (New York: Doubleday, 1976).

[5]*More New Games & Playful Ideas*, edited by Andrew Fluegelman (New York: Doubleday, 1981).

[6]Dale N. LeFevre, *New Games for the Whole Family* (New York: Putnam, 1988).

[7]*Fun Group Games for Children's Ministry* (Loveland, CO: Group Books, 1990).

[8]Ibid., 30.

CHAPTER 7

ADVENTUROUS ART AND CREATIVE CRAFTS

■ ■ ■ ■ ■ ■ ■ ■ ■ ■ ■ ■ ■ ■ ■ ■

BY MARY GRAY SWAN

Cliff was a 5-year-old terror in my group. Cliff had great diffi-culty relating to his peers. His anger would explode, and he would hit and kick. I got a lot of bruises trying to restrain him.

How could I help Cliff? I knew art experiences would help, but Cliff showed little interest. One day, I suggested Cliff try blotto painting (page 80). Cliff carefully dripped orange, green, yellow and black paint onto the paper, folded it shut and rubbed the out-side to spread the paint.

When Cliff opened his painting, his eyes grew wide. In each upper corner, mirroring each other, were two perfect pumpkins complete with green stems. "Look! Look!" he said. For a moment, Cliff found peace and joy. Through the blotto painting, I believe we both experienced grace.

Crafts are essential to a child's growth and development. Whether in Sunday school, vacation Bible school or an after-school program, children should have ample opportunity to explore and increase their creativity. Let children express their knowledge, thoughts and opinions in artistically creative ways.

Many teachers and leaders shy away from crafts because they feel they aren't "crafty" or creative. But since we're created in the image of God, I believe there's a creative spark within each one of us.

Just as gifts and talents vary from person to person, the level of creativity also varies. Some adults seem to have a creative instinct. Others need to learn to think creatively.

The Importance of Art and Creativity

How do you think creatively or encourage teachers to think creatively? Thinking creatively begins with looking for more than one way to do things. Thinking creatively means asking questions that have more than one answer. When you ask children the question, "How many different colors can you name in the sky today?" they'll look into the sky instead of just responding with the expected answer of "blue."

We must invite and encourage children to look for the unexpected, develop the skills of verbal description, explore options and feel the freedom to experiment with new ideas. When we do this, we're developing the creative side of children.

Enhancing a child's creative ability is to enhance the child's total development, including physical, mental, social, emotional and spiritual growth. A seemingly uncomplicated activity such as painting at an easel offers children several developmental opportunities. They develop eye-hand coordination as they dip their brushes in paint, make a mark on the paper and then manipulate the brush to make a design. They develop their small muscles as they control the brush with their fingers. They learn more about color, texture, shape, line and form. They interact with other children and learn social skills. They express their feelings through their design. And all of this may result in a deeper relationship with God as they express themselves.

Whew! A lot can happen with a seemingly "worthless" activity such as painting at an easel.

Doing Art With Children

How do you do arts and crafts with children? Don't just explain an art project and dump a bunch of art supplies on a child.

This can be overwhelming. Follow these 12 pointers:

1. Allow plenty of time. Don't rush the creative process.

2. Provide alternative activities for those who finish quickly. Some children work much more quickly than others.

3. Choose and prepare a good work space. Use bare floors or table tops that have plenty of elbowroom. Cover the work area with newspaper or oilcloth to make cleanup easier and to protect surfaces.

4. Be prepared. Children won't wait patiently while you gather materials or re-read instructions. *Always* try the craft first to see if it works and if you understand it.

5. Start by having children wash their hands. Cover the children's clothes with old shirts, smocks or aprons.

6. Work near water. If a sink isn't handy, have buckets of soapy and clear water nearby with a supply of towels.

7. Have children participate in cleanup. But before you assign specific cleanup tasks, know which children can do which tasks. Don't have an uncoordinated child clean up the paint. Set children up for success, not failure.

8. Never let children work with electrical appliances. Always carefully supervise any art activities that involve heat.

9. Choose activities that allow children to creatively express themselves. Vary activities by providing paper in various shapes and sizes. Give interesting backgrounds for children to work on such as cardboard, sandpaper, wood or fabric.

10. Use repetition. The same art activity can take on new form and meaning as a child grows and uses different materials. Consider combining two art projects such as chalk drawing and finger painting. Older children will stick with an art project longer and will be fascinated by the effects they create.

11. Affirm children. Make positive comments about the lines they draw, the forms they create, the colors they choose and the thought they've put into an art project. Avoid criticism. Don't touch up a child's artwork to "improve" it. And never ask, "What is it?"

12. Let the child be creative. Let children decide (within reasonable limits) how to use the art materials. Don't present a right and a wrong way to do an art project.

Essential Art Materials

You can offer a variety of creative art experiences to children of all ages as long as you have some basic supplies. These basics include:

● **Paper of all kinds**—construction paper, newsprint, manila paper, posterboard or tagboard, shelf paper or butcher paper.

● **Writing materials**—crayons, felt-tip markers (both broad and fine point), chalk and pencils.

● **Painting materials**—tempera paint, watercolors and paint-brushes.

● **Scissors**—for right- and left-handed children.

● **Adhesives**—white glue, tape and paste.

Add to your art supplies by asking for donations. Some children's ministers periodically send a list of needed supplies to the children's parents. On this list you might want to include: newspaper, wallpaper scraps, scrap paper from print shops, fabric scraps, buttons, other sewing trims, wrapping paper, ribbon, scraps of wire, yarn, magazines, catalogs, spools, egg cartons, empty toilet paper rolls and boxes.

Throughout the year, create crafts with these items. Then at the end of the year, consider using all the leftover materials for the kids to build a tower or some other structure.

If you have an adequate craft budget, you might want to buy aluminum foil, wax paper, clear and colored plastic wrap, lunch bags, paper plates, doilies, soda straws and modeling clay. I suggest you buy these items at discount stores or supermarkets where the prices will be considerably lower than at school-supply or office-supply stores.

CREATIVE IDEA

Colorful Adhesive

To make using glue more fun, add a couple of drops of food coloring to a bottle of white glue. Prepare four bottles of glue, each one in a different color: yellow, red, blue and green.

—L.B.—

Organizing Your Art Supplies

Once you have your art supplies, get organized. Attractively arrange basic supplies on shelves that are accessible to the children. Label the shelves so children can easily return unused materials to their proper places. For example, I put a picture of markers on the shelf (or box or can) where the markers go so even young children can easily find the space.

For art supplies you use only occasionally, sort, label and store them in an area that's convenient and accessible to the teacher. Too many teachers forget about art supplies that are tucked away in unlabeled bags or boxes in the back of closets and cabinets.

Consider using baskets, bins, trays and clear plastic boxes to organize art supplies. Recyclables also work well. Clear plastic peanut butter jars can hold small items such as beads and buttons. Use plastic ketchup and syrup bottles to mix powdered tempera paints. Pie pans and plastic frozen-dinner trays are ideal for holding miscellaneous art supplies.

Large churches often designate a supply room for teachers. Consider having a volunteer in charge of the supply room to keep the room organized and to order supplies when they run low. Each Sunday, this person can also gather all the materials each teacher needs and put each teacher's materials into a plastic carry-all (which you can find for about $3 at a discount store in the housewares section).

Small churches may store supplies in each Sunday school room. Or one church has a small supply room that's kept locked. But teachers can access it any time since the key is hidden nearby.

Art With a Conscience

Once you start collecting supplies, you'll quickly become a "pack rat." Before you throw away anything, you'll ask yourself if you can use it for an art project. Not only is this good stewardship, but children will learn from your example that they shouldn't mindlessly throw things away.

An area that concerns me is wasting food in creative art. Some programming resources suggest activities that waste large amounts of food for no good reason. I have reservations about this practice even though it is popular.

If you're interested, a creative alternative to using food is often easy to find. For example, instead of vegetable printing, use kitchen utensils, keys, combs, blocks, rollers or soap.

Age-Appropriate Arts and Crafts

I've categorized the following art activities by age level. Although the crafts for older children are inappropriate for preschoolers, the opposite isn't true. So-called preschool crafts have intergenerational appeal.

Preschoolers

● **Blotto**—Prefold art paper in half and reopen. Have children each randomly drip a small amount of tempera paint onto the paper, using different colors for more colorful art. Have them each close the paper and gently rub the outside to spread the paint on the inside, then open to reveal a mirrored design.

● **Spatter painting**—Have children each lay an object such as a leaf on a piece of paper. Hold a piece of screen above the paper. Have them dip a toothbrush or vegetable brush in tempera paint and gently brush over the screen so the paint spatters onto the paper below, then remove the object.

● **Crayon melting**—Place a piece of wax paper (about 12" long) on top of a pad of newspaper. Have children scrape crayon shavings from several colors of old crayons onto the wax paper with a dull knife. Have them each fold the wax paper in half with the shavings on the inside and cover the wax paper with a paper towel. Then have an adult iron with a warm iron. The crayon shavings will melt together to look like stained glass. Then have children cut the wax papers into shapes or frame them with construction paper.

● **Bubble painting**—Secure a large piece of butcher paper on a fence or between two poles. Add several drops of food coloring to bubble-blowing liquid. Let children blow bubbles in the direction of the paper. Then use the paper as gift wrap for gifts to parents or as the background for a bulletin board.

MONEY–SAVING TIP

Easy Art Supply Recipes

Finger Paint
½ cup Argo laundry starch
2 cups water
1 personal-size bar Ivory soap, grated
¼ cup talcum powder
1 teaspoon oil of cloves, sassafras or peppermint as preservative

In a saucepan, dissolve starch in a little water to make a paste. Add remaining water and cook slowly until mixture becomes glossy and clear, stirring constantly to avoid lumping. Let the starch cool. Beat in remaining ingredients. Store in an airtight container. Add powdered or liquid tempera at the time of the activity for color.

Modeling Dough
4 cups flour
2 cups salt
4 cups water
8 teaspoons cream of tartar
4 tablespoons cooking oil
food coloring

Thoroughly mix all ingredients. Cook over medium heat, stirring constantly until mixture thickens and leaves side of pot. Turn onto counter top. Knead. When cool, store in an airtight container.

—M.S.—

Grades K-3

● **Leaf pounding**—Arrange green leaves on a piece of wood or Masonite. Place a piece of unbleached muslin, heavyweight interfacing or a similar light-color fabric over the leaves. Secure with tape at the edges so the fabric won't move. Gently hammer the fabric with a mallet until the chlorophyll from the leaves comes through onto the fabric.

● **Melted-crayon painting**—Remove paper from old crayons and sort colors into muffin tins or small metal containers such as cat-food cans or pudding cans. Cover the bottom and sides of an electric frying pan with aluminum foil for protection. Then place crayon cups in the frying pan. Turn on a low setting and allow the crayons to melt. Give children each a work surface such as cardboard, heavy

IN-DEPTH INFORMATION

Crafts for All Ages

You can do basic creative activities with children of all ages. Descriptions, needed materials, procedures and age adaptations appear below:

Activity	Materials	Procedure	Age Adaptations
Drawing	Use different kinds of paper, crayons, pencils, felt-tip markers and colored pencils.	Let children do this while sitting on the floor or at a table.	Expect only scribbles from toddlers. Older children may enjoy combining media.
Brush painting	Use 18×24 paper, tempera paint and brushes of assorted widths.	Have children do this at easels or on the table or floor.	Use only one or two colors at a time for young children.
Finger painting	Use a Formica counter top, cookie sheet or cafeteria tray; finger paint; powdered tempera; and large sheets of butcher paper or newsprint.	Let children paint directly on the counter top, cookie sheet or tray. When finished, lay a piece of paper over the finger paint to make a picture.	This art activity works well with all ages. Let even 2-year-olds fin-gerpaint on the surface.
Chalking	Use manila or construction paper, colored and white chalk and hair spray.	Have children dip chalk in water for a different effect. Have an adult spray the pic-ture with hair spray, which keeps the art from smudging.	Expect only scribbles from young children. Combine chalk-ing with finger painting for older children.

Activity	Materials	Procedure	Age Adaptations
Collage	Use cardboard or paper plates for background material. Provide paper scraps, magazines, fabric scraps and glue.	Let children arrange items on their background materials as they wish.	Pour glue into butter lids and let young children dip items in the glue, then place the items on the background paper.
Modeling dough or clay	Use dough or clay. Consider providing sculpting tools.	Let children manipulate as desired.	Modeling dough or clay is difficult for young children.

—M.S.—

paper, tree bark or a piece of scrap wood. Use cotton swabs to paint the melted crayon wax onto the work surface. The crayon will harden when it hits the work surface, but it will leave a texture.

Grades 4-6

● **Ping-Pong-ball painting**—Cover a large surface with butcher paper. Dip Ping-Pong balls into liquid tempera paint and play "Keep the Ball on the Table." Drop the paint-covered balls onto the middle of the paper and have children blow the balls around. Use the final product for a tablecloth, a bulletin board background or wrapping paper.

● **Juice-can lid ornaments**—Save lids from frozen fruit-juice cans until you have at least one per child. Cut a circle the same size as the lid out of paper for each child. Have children draw a design on the paper. Give each child a juice-can lid, a block of wood, a nail and a hammer. Lightly attach the paper design to the lid with rubber cement. Have children gently tap holes through the paper into the lid at even, but short intervals (about ¼ inch) until the design is completed. Remove the pattern. Punch a final hole in the top of the lid. Hang with ribbon or yarn.

CHAPTER 8

MAKING MUSIC WITH CHILDREN

■ ■ ■ ■ ■ ■ ■ ■ ■ ■ ■ ■ ■ ■

BY MARGARET RICKERS HINCHEY

Music opens up new worlds for children. I see how important music is as I walk through the oncology ward of Children's Hospital in Denver. A parent pulls his 5-year-old son in a wagon with an I.V. pole looming overhead. Next to the little boy sits a stuffed collie that plays AM and FM music. As I walk by the play area, a blond 6-year-old girl, balding because of chemotherapy, plays a colorful xylophone. Across the hall a child watches a music video.

At the nurses station, the radio is tuned to a local classical music station. In the next room a mother rocks her infant to sleep as she quietly sings a lullaby. In the therapy room down the hall, recorded music motivates children to learn to crawl, walk and talk.

Music calms children's spirits. It relaxes children and fills a void in many lives. But music is more. It can motivate a child or entertain. Music can teach. And it can be an expression of faith.

Music Helps Children Express Their Faith

Children are expressive. They wear their emotions every day. Often children find it difficult to express those emotions and their faith in appropriate ways. Part of the problem is that faith is an abstract concept, making it hard for children to grasp.

Music can be the answer, since music makes faith real and concrete. It helps kids express their faith in a fun way. Children can experience faith through musical instruments, choirs and hymns. Songs such as "Jesus Loves Me" and "For God So Loved the World" give children concrete ways to share their faith with their friends and families.

Music can also function as a memory trigger. In teaching a class of fourth-graders in vacation Bible school, I asked the class to write 1 John 4:7-8 from memory. As the children wrote, I heard humming in the room. In my typical teacher style, I asked for silence during the quiz. Silence prevailed for about 30 seconds, then the humming began again.

I moved around the room slowly and finally stopped at the seat of Vicki, the source of the humming. "Vicki," I said, "I've asked you to be quiet. Why are you still humming?"

With a frustrated look on her face, she replied, "Well, I learned that Bible verse by singing a song. Every time I get to one part you ask us to be quiet, and I have to start over again. I'll never be able to write down the whole Bible verse unless I can sing it to myself."

Vicki had used music as a tool for memorization. And today Vicki is a teacher. When I saw her recently, she assured me she remembered the incident. And she can still sing 1 John 4:7-8.

Several years ago General Foods chose Johann Sebastian Bach's "Prelude and Fugue in D Minor" as background music for one of its Jell-O commercials. One Sunday, I played that Bach composition as a prelude in church. As I began the familiar opening chords of the piece, an excited 5-year-old told his mother: "Listen, Mom! Margaret's playing the Jell-O song!"

Everyone Can Be Musical

A member of our church told me last week: "I can't sing a note, but I sure do love to hear those children sing in church. It makes me feel good." Not everyone has the gift of singing, but children and adults can be involved in music in other ways.

There are three ways to be involved in music: listening, participating and sharing. Just because someone can't sing doesn't mean he or she can't listen and appreciate good music. Almost every child will listen to music, but some may hesitate to participate—and may totally balk at performing. Don't push children so hard that they eventually dislike music. Instead, use fun songs kids enjoy to encourage their participating. Affirm children's interest at any level.

In contrast you may have children who constantly sing, whistle, hum, pound on the piano or "perform" for anyone who will listen. These children need to understand the difference between performing and participating. Participating includes everything from hand clapping to singing a simple melody to playing an instrument. Performance involves publicly sharing your God-given musical gifts and talents. Children need to understand that performance involves sharing a talent, not showing it off. And performance requires lots of practice.

Creative Music Ideas

In your children's ministry, music can play a significant role—beyond just singing songs. Tune in to these 10 ideas:

1. If children are extremely excited or unmanageable, play music with a slow tempo. It will help quell their emotions.

2. Play peppy music to lift children from their doldrums if they seem tired and lethargic.

3. As children enter the classroom, have classical music playing in the background. This exposes children to the "masters." Children may even develop some musical awareness. Or use other background music of your preference.

4. Play a familiar song, such as "Row, Row, Row Your Boat," and ask older kids to write new lyrics to fit a theme such as Easter

or Thanksgiving or a Bible story such as the good Samaritan.

5. With younger children, use action songs or finger plays with music to illustrate a story.

6. Use songs to help children learn each other's names. Many music books have songs that incorporate children's names.

7. Use clapping, dancing or other actions to give children a break from the routine.

8. Use music to reinforce learning. For example, I remember the story of Zacchaeus climbing the sycamore tree because I sang it so often in my Sunday school classes as a child.

9. Help kids memorize with music. Some music books have songs based on the psalms and other Bible verses. You can find songs based on the Lord's Prayer and the names of all the Bible books.

10. Use music to help children develop good listening skills. Ask children to listen to music and identify repetitive phrases, notes that sound good together or notes that are dissonant (sound bad to them).

Leading Children's Music

Many people who work with children are talented, but they don't know how to play a musical instrument or carry a tune. That doesn't mean they can't lead children's music! Help your non-musical volunteers develop children's musical talent by:

CREATIVE IDEA

Making Music With Preschoolers

Preschoolers enjoy singing and being active. So put their singing voices and active bodies into action at the same time.

When singing a song such as "Jesus Loves Me," have the children sing the song five times. The first time have the children crouch near the ground and sing the song as quietly as they can. Each time they sing the song, have the children stand up a little bit more and sing the verse a little bit louder. By the fifth time, children should be jumping up and down and singing as loudly as they can without shouting or screaming.

—J.R.—

● Asking a church musician to record several songs to use with children. Have the musician record a song in several different musical styles. For example, have the musician play the music on a keyboard. Then have him or her play the music and sing the words. Then have the musician play the music one line at a time so children can learn the music little by little.

● Inviting one of your church musicians or choir members to visit the classroom periodically. The musician can teach the children a new song or expose the children to a new instrument.

● Asking older children who play a musical instrument or who like to sing to lead a song.

● Inviting a parent with musical ability to come regularly to lead music. Some parents may even play the bagpipes!

● Finding commercial songleading tapes and records. Most Christian bookstores have these musical resources. For older children, check out *The Group Songbook*.[1]

Making Music Fun for Children

Although music is an expression of faith and an educational tool, it's also a lot of fun. So sometimes do music just for the fun of it! Children of different ages can have fun with music in different ways:

● **Nursery**—Use musical toys such as xylophones, drums, rattles, guitars, trumpets and keyboards to create a children's band. In my experience, it's better to use commercially made toys instead of homemade instruments with this age. Toddlers can easily choke on the pieces inside a homemade rattle if it falls apart.

Play recorded music and ask the children to play their instruments. Tell them to stop playing when the music stops. Play the music softly and ask the children to play softly. Then play the music loudly and have the children play loudly.

● **Preschoolers**—Have children make homemade musical instruments. Use glasses with colored water at different levels to make tonal sounds. Staple together paper plates with dried beans inside for tambourines. Use round oatmeal boxes as drums. Use potato chip cylinders with plastic lids, filled with dried beans, to make shakers. Preschoolers will take pride in their creations as

IN-DEPTH INFORMATION

Meaningful Music for All Ages

Age	Participation	Music Education	Appropriate Music
Nursery (1- and 2-year-olds)	● Clap; older children will show a sense of rhythm ● Repeat short musical phrases	● Recognize music that is loud or soft ● Learn to clap or tap	● Simple one-line responses
Preschool (3- to 5-year-olds)	● Clap and march in rhythm to music ● Recognize familiar songs ● Repeat longer phrases, especially refrains to songs ● Memorize nursery rhyme songs and simple religious songs	● Recognize music that is high, low, slow or fast ● Clap or tap in rhythm to music	● Nursery rhymes ● Repetitious refrains
Lower Elementary (K-3)	● Clap on command (for example, as indicated periodically in a song) ● Sing in a choir with other children ● Repeat more difficult songs that may not include repetition ● Maintain a melody while others sing or play in harmony ● Begin to develop skills on keyboard instruments	● Replicate notes in a scale ● Recognize and repeat intervals ● Recognize whole, half, quarter and eighth notes by grade 3 ● Do simple sight singing	● Simple songs or hymns within an octave and one-half range with repetition

Age	Participation	Music Education	Appropriate Music
Upper Elementary (4-6)	• Learn to play band or orchestral instruments (most school programs begin in the fourth or fifth grade) • Sing more difficult choral pieces or hymns with vocal quality • Memorize almost any songs with words at their reading level • Sing in harmony with other voices	• Execute more complex rhythmic patterns • Learn to sing intervals at sight • Read key and time signatures • Accomplish two-part sight singing	• Two-part songs with harmony

—M.H.—

well as the "joyful noise" they make with them.

Play familiar songs and have children sing and play along with the music. Have them practice the song fast and then slow.

● **K-3**—Teach children songs that incorporate their names. For example, "Jesus in the Morning" from *Sing 'n' Celebrate for Kids!* [2] has simple words you can adapt to fit the children's names. Sing the song through first with the "Jesus" words. Then go around the room and have children each sing out their name when it's their turn. For example: "Susan, Jennifer, Jason in the morning, Dustin at the noontime. Alex, Stephanie, Julie when the sun goes down." Repeat the song until all the children have been "sung" at least once. Children love to hear their names in a song!

● **Grades 4-6**—A great educational tool that's fun for children in this age group is Musical Bingo. Although commercial versions of this game are available, you can make (or have the children make) your own version of this game. Instead of B-I-N-G-O across the top of the cards, write M-U-S-I-C. For columns, use a sharp sign; flat sign; treble clef sign; bass clef sign; different key signa-tures; and symbols for soft, loud, crescendo and decrescendo. Play the game like any bingo game with a caller, players marking their cards and the first one to complete a column winning.

Notes
■ ■ ■ ■

[1]*The Group Songbook*, edited by Paul Woods and Cindy Sauer (Loveland, CO: Group Books, 1991).

[2]*Sing 'n' Celebrate for Kids* (Waco, TX: Word, Inc., 1977).

CHAPTER 9

PRESENTATIONS WITH A PURPOSE

■ ■ ■ ■ ■ ■ ■ ■ ■ ■ ■ ■ ■ ■ ■

BY DALE AND LIZ VONSEGGEN

The key to working with children is *variety*. Any good teaching method can become routine if overworked. Therefore you must always look for creative ways to teach children.

Using a lot of different teaching methods adds an element of surprise to your children's ministry. Children become more interested. They guess what will happen next.

Repetition is important to help kids learn, so use a variety of methods to teach the same concept. If you want children to learn that Jesus loves them, for example, teach it over and over again by using music, a story, an object lesson, a game, memorization and role-play—all in one lesson!

So how can you creatively present information to children? Chapters 5 to 8 give in-depth information on active learning, games, crafts and music. This chapter explores five other presentation methods: puppets, storytelling, clowning, drama and illusions.

Puppets With a Purpose

One of the most dynamic teaching tools is a hand puppet with a moving mouth. Of course, you can use different kinds of puppets, but *Sesame Street* has trained children to expect puppets with moving mouths.

You don't need a lot of expertise to use puppets. You can buy a commercially made puppet and have the puppet lip-sync to a song played on a nearby tape recorder. As you gain experience, you can eventually write your own scripts and create different voices.

Whether you're a veteran puppeteer or a first-timer, it's important to know the basics. Open the puppet's mouth once for each syllable spoken. Be sure the eyes of the puppet look at the audience. Make sure the audience can see the puppet's body, arms and head.

In addition to knowing the basics of operating puppets, it's important to gear puppetry to the audience's age. Some approaches that work well with older children don't always work well with young children, and vice versa. We've found the following methods to be effective for the different ages:

● **Preschoolers**—With preschoolers, use soft, touchable puppets to assist you as another voice in the classroom. It's amazing how much more attentive preschoolers are when a teacher says something and a friendly puppet agrees. Create a personality for the puppet that differs from your own. If possible, give the puppet a cutesy voice that children will enjoy listening to.

For preschoolers, action and repetition are more important than clever, funny scripts. Adapt nursery rhymes or familiar tunes for the puppet to use in teaching children some basic lessons.

For example, we've created various messages to the tune of "The Farmer in the Dell." One message that works with the tune is: "I like you. I like you. I want a lot of friends, so I like you!" Another message: "Roses are red. Daisies are white. Let's take turns and never fight!" Or sing: "Roses are red. Grass is green. It's not nice to hit or be mean."

One Christmas we had 3- and 4-year-olds each make lambs by stuffing a lunch sack with newspaper, closing the end with a rubber band and covering the bag with cotton balls. We also used medium-size sacks with one side cut out to make shepherds' headpieces for each child to wear.

MONEY-SAVING TIP

5 Inexpensive Puppet Stages

You don't need to buy an elaborate, expensive puppet stage to present your puppet shows. Even if you have zero dollars in your budget, you can still put on a puppet show. Try these ideas:

1. Have two people hold a blanket between them to create a stage.
2. Turn a table on its side.
3. Cut a window in a refrigerator box. Paint the box to look like a TV set.
4. In summer, string rope between two trees about 3 feet from the ground. Hang a dark sheet or blanket over the rope.
5. Have a carpenter build a wooden stage that has hinges so you can fold it up. (Use pine or paneling so it won't be too heavy.)

—D.V. and L.V.—

The children walked around the room carrying their lambs, searching for green pasture. When they got to a predetermined spot, an angel puppet appeared over the side of a "hill" and told them all about the baby Jesus born in Bethlehem. The children sure remembered that story!

Other ways to use puppets with preschoolers include:

● Use knock-knock jokes.

● Have puppets ask children yes-and-no questions.

● Have children clap or raise their hands if they hear the puppet make a mistake when saying a Bible verse or singing a song they know.

● Invite preschoolers to sing along with the puppet or sing a song for the puppet.

● K-3—With this age group, use a puppet as a guest in your classroom. Dress the puppet as a Bible character or visitor from another country. Have the children ask the puppet questions.

Consider using a puppet to help with discipline. When discipline problems occur, have the puppet tell the children what went wrong. If done sensitively, the puppet's rapport with the children allows it to address the issue more freely without hurting feelings.

A puppet can be a great storyteller or contribute to the story the teacher tells. The puppet is something fun and colorful for the children to watch, and a puppet can confirm lesson truths for children.

BY THE WAY, I WON'T BE NEEDING THIS LITTLE TEACHER'S PACKET OF HELPS... I'VE FOUND THAT MOST CHILDREN ENJOY STRAIGHT LECTURE.

CREATIVE IDEA

Storing Puppets

Take advantage of discarded hat boxes, bags, a file cabinet or another container to house your puppets so children can't see or play with the puppets until you're ready to use them.

—L.V. and D.V.—

Children at this age also enjoy repeating their memory work for a special puppet. Think about having a professor puppet or a wise owl for children to tell what they learned.

● **Grades 4-6**—With older children, use puppets to play games. For example, play 20 Questions with a puppet where kids must ask 20 yes-or-no questions to figure out the person, place or event the puppet has chosen. The child who guesses the correct answer becomes the next puppeteer.

Have a puppet comment on how kids are doing at a craft or project. Or have a puppet who is a "cool" musician, disc jockey, guitar player or drummer lead the singing.

Children at this age can also make puppets and write their own scripts. Have them present puppet shows to younger children in your church.

Secrets of Storytelling

According to Mark 4:2, Jesus' frequent method of teaching was telling stories. So why not follow his example in teaching children today? Storytelling seems simple. But make your storytelling most effective with children by doing the following:

● **Maintain eye contact.** Look directly into the eyes of your audience. Make people feel you understand what they're thinking as you tell the story.

● **Paint pictures.** Let your listeners visualize the characters by the way you describe them. Show drawings or visuals as often as you can. Children remember better when they hear *and* see.

● **Use sound effects.** Children love to hear how various characters speak. Create a grouch by the way you use your voice. Make the sound of the wind or the sea or animals. Actually cry, yell, sneeze or stutter if it adds to the story. You'll capture kids' attention, especially very young children.

● **Incorporate variety.** Speak softly at times, then loudly, depending on what's happening in the story. Pause for suspense or surprise. When the action becomes exciting, talk more rapidly. When emphasizing a lesson at the end of a story, present it slowly. Consider repeating it.

Here are specific ways to use storytelling with different age groups:

● **Preschoolers**—When telling stories to young children, use large picture books so children can see what's happening as the teacher tells the story.

MONEY-SAVING TIP

Transform Garbage Into Storytelling Props

Visuals often printed in teachers guides or teaching aids can be made into stand-up characters for storytelling. Simply tape the two-dimensional figures to something you usually throw away: empty toilet paper rolls or paper towel tubes. Have the "tube" people in the story move and interact with other characters. After telling the story, give the characters to the children to use as they retell the story.

—L.V. and D.V.—

Visuals are crucial for this age group. If you don't have a picture book to tell a story, make visual story cards with bright colors. Have preschoolers actually participate in the story.

For example, in telling the story of feeding the 5,000, have children walk in place as if they were going to the mountainside. Next, describe how people felt when they saw Jesus. Have the children jump up and down because they're so happy. Then have the children sit to listen.

During the story have the children act out getting sleepy by lying down and closing their eyes. Further on during the story, have the children get hungry and rub their tummies. Tell the entire story, leading the motions.

In telling a story about Joseph, have children clap and smile when something good happens to Joseph. When something bad happens, have the children hold their heads in their hands, shake their heads and say, "Oh, no!"

● **K-3**—Object lessons are wonderful attention-getting stories for children of this age. But make sure the lessons are concrete and easy to understand. A lot of object lessons teach abstract concepts children won't understand. For example, the biblical concept that we are "the salt of the earth" is too abstract for children of this age. Even sprinkling salt on a globe or having kids taste salt sprinkled into their palms will not enable kids to understand this concept. Their concrete mental capacities will still lead them to questions such as, "How can I get into a salt shaker?" Use age-appropriate concrete concepts such as God's love, forgiveness, prayer or gifts.

CREATIVE IDEA

Using Hats and Masks in Storytelling

Use a variety of hats to indicate different characters in a story. For example, in a story about prayer, children who say prayer involves memorized lines wear beanies. Wearing hard hats, children act as construction workers who say prayer is hard work. Flowery hats adorn their heads when they act like old women who say prayer is as sweet as a rose.

Masks also can depict different characters. We especially like half masks because they don't muffle words. Use masks to portray the devil, a sailor (for Jonah) or a lion (to tell the story of Daniel in the lion's den from the lion's perspective). A mask makes the story more real to children.

—L.V. and D.V.—

Children at this age love having stories read to them. Use short children's books or check out the stories written for children in devotional books for families.

Have children participate in stories. They can do more sophisticated actions than preschoolers. For example, consider using mops and brooms made into stick puppets. As you tell the story, some children move the puppets while other children do sound effects as you cue them.

● **Grades 4-6**—Use Bible charades to involve fourth- to sixth-graders in your story. Provide ideas and props for one or two children to silently act out a story while the rest of the class guesses who the characters are and what happened in the story.

Some good scripture stories for children to act out include:

● 1 Samuel 16:1-13, where David is chosen to be king after Saul;

● 1 Kings 17, where the widow of Zarephath gives away her last bit of food;

● Luke 5:1-9, where Peter's obedience to Jesus results in catching lots of fish; and

● Acts 16:16-34, where Paul and Silas—jailed for preaching about Jesus—win the jailer to Christ.

Object lessons work well with this age group. In fact, children at this age enjoy being given an object and making up their own lesson. These children are particularly interested in object lessons with surprise endings—or ones that have a chemical reaction or optical illusion. It's important, though, to keep the object lessons concrete and specific.

An ineffective object lesson would be to hold a rock up and say, "Jesus is our rock." Kids this age may have difficulty conceptualizing that this means he is our steadfast and strong savior. They may think he is a literal rock. It would be better to take children to a large rock or boulder, and have them push against it. Afterward, say, "The Bible says Jesus is like a rock. What does that mean?" Be specific in helping children understand this abstract concept.

You can also involve children in stories by having them illustrate a story as you tell it. Have children all do this at the same time or have one child draw in front of the group on a flip chart or blackboard. Children love to watch a peer draw.

Ministering With Clowns

Clowns make children laugh. Smile. Snicker. Clowns can captivate a child without saying a word. And a clown can teach a lesson a child will never forget.

Clowning involves more than donning a clown costume and putting on clown makeup. Develop a purpose for your character. The clown should demonstrate a child-like faith and act with God-like acceptance of everyone. This character should give away love and share joy when interacting with children.

Floyd Shaffer, the authority in Christian clown ministry, has written the best resources available for clown ministry (see Resources for Children's Ministry, pages 219-223). To use clowns in your ministry, be sensitive to the developmental differences of children of different ages.

● **Preschoolers**—Maintain a distance from young children and gesture your greeting. If you see a favorable response, you may move closer, but be prepared to move away if your clown frightens a child. Preschool children often fear a white-faced or highly animated clown.

Don't think you always have to wear the entire clowning garb with children this age. Consider doing a skit with just a clown hat or red nose. Large clown props such as a comb, toothbrush or fluffy bath towel will capture children's attention.

● **K-3**—Clowns make good greeters to shake hands or pat heads of children coming to class. Have a clown create interest in a subject. For example, give the clown a treasure chest labeled "World's Greatest Treasure." As a child comes close to peek, have the clown open the lid to show a picture of Jesus inside.

Children at this age may enjoy face painting. Paint different faces that reflect different moods such as happiness, sadness, worry or fear. Have an entire group of children express actions and show feelings with their faces and bodies as you tell a story.

Children also love parades. Create a parade of children with clowns to promote an upcoming event such as vacation Bible school. Have children parade into a worship service with the clowns to make an announcement. Or have children parade through a neighborhood, local mall or the church's Sunday school classes.

● **Grades 4-6**—By the time children become fourth- to sixth-graders, they enjoy watching clown skits, especially if they don't have to become too involved in the skits.

Children may antagonize a clown by stepping on his toes, pulling his nose or stealing his props. A clown must be prepared with clever visual tools such as magic objects. Remember, a clown shouldn't retaliate with evil but with kindness.

Sixth-graders may enjoy becoming part of a clown ministry team. If you have interested kids, teach them how to correctly put on clown makeup, to develop a clown character and to do skits to be presented to their peers or younger children.

A team of sixth-grade clowns can also provide an important ministry by visiting children in the hospital. Have clowns minister by waving, blowing kisses, giving away cheery get-well cards. Or have clowns visit local retirement communities or nursing homes.

Drama: The Dramatic Teacher

Dramatization of Bible events is a powerful tool for learning because children can more easily identify with people on stage than with people described in a book. Drama has many forms—from simple role-plays to full-scale dramatic productions that include memorizing scripts, wearing costumes and building sets.

Use drama in different ways, depending on the age of the children in your ministry.

● **Preschoolers**—Doing drama with 3- to 5-year-olds should be simple, simple, simple. Have preschoolers wave palm branches while singing about Palm Sunday. Or have children pretend they're fishermen when you tell the story about Jesus telling Peter where to catch lots of fish. Children can pretend to throw nets into the sea and pull out a net full of fish.

Young children also enjoy simple role-plays, as long as they can act and not speak (although some young children are willing to do sound effects). For example, as the teacher tells the parable of the sower, have preschoolers each act like a farmer with a bag of seeds on their shoulder. Have children walk in a straight line pretending to plant seeds along a row as they walk.

Another way to use drama with preschoolers is to have them be "still" actors in a larger dramatic presentation that includes older children. Have preschoolers wear costumes and give them poses to act in the "frozen picture." The nativity scene works well with preschoolers.

● **K-3**—Bible pantomimes are a fun way for children of this age to present a lesson to the class. Give one or two props to the children doing the pantomime. Suggest several gestures or actions you want them to present. Encourage children to exaggerate the actions so their peers can more easily guess the characters they're pantomiming and what the story is about.

Children at this age can be rather creative at role-playing.

Assign each child a definite character. Explain how the story begins and ends, and let the children create what the characters say. It might be helpful to read aloud the Bible story before the children act it out.

Interviews are another type of dramatization, but you need to give children at this age a lot of guidance. Provide questions and answers for those taking part. For example, one child may dress up as Paul. Children can ask Paul questions (which Paul would already have the answers for). When children enjoy this type of dramatization, they eventually feel more comfortable ad-libbing the parts.

● **Grades 4-6**—Older children especially enjoy the dramatization technique known as readers theater. The teacher prepares a script ahead of time with narrator and actor parts. The children use only their voices to act. They may speak slowly, quickly, loudly or softly and use their voices in other ways. Sometimes, several actors may speak lines together, such as the theme of the readers theater—"Love your enemies" for example. The actors stand in a row at the front of the room or sit on stools. Whenever a child appears in a scene, he or she faces the audience. In a scene where the child isn't present, he or she faces away from the audience.

Fourth- to sixth-graders are quite good at mimicking well-known characters such as reporters and famous people. After presenting a lesson, ask children to write a few sentences to summarize the lesson and then present the information as if they were a famous person such as the president, a reporter, a movie star or a singer.

Don't overlook full-scale plays or musicals. These require a lot of work, but some children really enjoy them. Have kids make props and scenery, prepare posters, design the program, sing, act or make costumes. Such an activity can benefit not only the audience but also the children involved. Full-scale dramas can build community in your group.

Illusions: Memorable Presentations

In some circles, the term "magic" is associated with the occult. However, there's nothing wrong with the element of surprise or the unexpected. Jesus did the unexpected when he told Peter to catch a fish. Of course, this wasn't magic, but a miracle. Though we can't perform miracles like Jesus did, we can create illusions to demonstrate truths.

Over the years children have enjoyed lessons we've presented using chemical reactions to demonstrate truths. For example, one

---

WORKSHEET

Planning a Creative Presentation

Before the Presentation

Lesson Topic: _____

Scripture: _____

Creative techniques you plan to use: _____

_____

_____

Materials required: _____

_____

Senses the creative presentation will include:

_____ Sight _____ Sound _____ Smell _____ Taste _____ Touch

Time needed for presentation: _____

Actual time used: _____

After the Presentation

Children's attention: EXCELLENT   GOOD   FAIR   POOR

Children's comments: _____

_____

Spontaneous additions that occurred during the presentation: _____

_____

Suggestions for improvement: _____

_____

Where presentation materials are stored: _____

_____

—L.V. and D.V.—

tablespoon of white vinegar mixed in three tablespoons of water will bubble up and foam over the edge of a glass when you stir a teaspoonful of baking soda into the water. The same soda stirred into plain water will not react. We use this illusion to demonstrate that we can't see sin inside a person, but when a person acts on the sin, everyone can see it.

Daring to Be Creative

This chapter only presented a few ideas on how to make creative presentations to children. They should get you started or get you thinking about new ways to teach children.

You don't need to be extremely creative to try something new. You just need to be daring. Dare to try something new—something outside your comfort zone. Use common objects in uncommon ways. Jesus used a boy's lunch and a fig tree to teach important lessons.

So be brave. Look for new ways to teach children. Dress up a broom as a Bible character to talk to your class. Have children present a story using balloons they've decorated as people. The possibilities are endless. And the possibilities will make learning a lot more fun and memorable for children.

Part Three:
Age-Specific Ministries

CHAPTER 10

THE POWER OF PRENATAL MINISTRY

■ ■ ■ ■ ■ ■ ■ ■ ■ ■ ■ ■ ■ ■ ■ ■

BY VICKI ASHCRAFT

A s I passed the boys bathroom one Sunday morning, I heard a father yell at his 2-year-old boy for not sitting still during the pastor's sermon. I wanted to burst into the bathroom and tell the father what I thought. A 2-year-old *can't* sit still during the pastor's sermon!

As I stood by the bathroom door, I realized my other frustrations. Some parents in our church thought our nursery was a free baby-sitting service. And certain parents—like this father—didn't have good parenting skills. Although we had parenting classes, few came.

What was wrong with our children's ministry? After mulling over the situation and praying about it, I realized the problem: Having a children's ministry that starts with nursery is too late. It must start sooner.

Why Minister to an Unborn Child?

I began researching to find out what takes place in the womb and the critical role a church can play during this time. I discovered that several major universities are doing research on the unborn child. And I realized what an important time pregnancy is for expectant parents. A book by Dr. Thomas Verny, *The Secret Life of the Unborn Child*, opened my eyes. I learned:

● A fetus can hear clearly from about the sixth month. Dr. Henry Truby, professor of pediatrics at the University of Miami, learned that fetuses even move in rhythm to their mother's speech. Play Vivaldi, and the unborn child relaxes; play Beethoven, and the fetus kicks and moves.[1]

● The mother's attitude has the greatest effect on how an infant turns out, says psychologist Dr. Monika Lukesch of Constantine University in Frankfurt, West Germany. Women who look forward to having a child have healthier babies than mothers with unwanted pregnancies.[2]

● The quality of the expectant mother's relationship with her spouse—or the man who helped her conceive—was the second most important factor in determining a child's outcome, Lukesch found.[3]

During pregnancy, people want to be good parents. Expectant parents usually ask a lot of questions on how to train a child. Most expectant parents don't know where to look for good materials. What an ideal time for the church to train people on how to be parents—before they're parents.

IN-DEPTH INFORMATION

Parenting Starts at Conception

The way mothers treat themselves during pregnancy is the beginning of their parenting. The way they treat themselves affects their children.

● Babies with fetal alcohol syndrome are born to women who abuse alcohol during their pregnancy. One out of 250 babies is born with fetal alcohol syndrome. The incidence is 30 times higher in Native American babies.[4]

● Although the median family income for Hispanics is 36 percent lower than for whites, their infant death rate is lower than whites. Why? Researcher Fernando Trevino of the University of Texas Medical Branch, Galveston, says Hispanic expectant mothers have better diets, rarely smoke, are rarely single and have strong extended families.[5]

—J.R.—

Not only are people interested in being parents during pregnancy, but they have a lot more time. After birthing, new parents get caught in the cycle of feeding and changing a baby every two hours. It's a stressful time, and if parents don't have parenting knowledge ahead of time, they're going to wing it. And they may end up like the father who chewed out his son for not sitting still during the sermon. They just won't understand.

The Benefits of a Prenatal Ministry

Many young couples don't regularly attend church. Yes, young couples are busy, but many times they don't get regularly involved in church because the church doesn't have anything to offer. In our church, our prenatal ministry shows how committed our church is to young families.

By meeting the needs of expectant parents, a prenatal ministry can develop a bond between young parents and the church. And this kind of ministry often ensures the church will treat all couples equally. Otherwise it's easy for a church to throw a baby shower for a married couple and not do anything for a single parent who accidentally got pregnant.

Spiritual growth also happens in a prenatal ministry. Many unchurched couples have started coming to our church because of our prenatal ministry. Baby showers and baby dedications have attracted people who would've never come to one of our church services.

Since the inception of our prenatal ministry, we've received a benefit that we never imagined. Many couples who've gone through the prenatal ministry volunteer to help other expectant parents. They want to share the same benefits they received with another couple.

Elements of Prenatal Ministry

A prenatal ministry can include a variety of elements. Here are some that have been effective in our church:

● **Prenatal partners**—Assign each expectant family a church partner—either a husband-and-wife team or a single person. This partner becomes the family's primary contact and support, praying for the family, making sure the family receives resources, and helping the family as needed.

Give each prenatal partner a job description and a qualification sheet to fill out. Also require monthly reports from partners to ensure they are carrying out the ministry and not neglecting the family.

In our congregation, some partners have helped families clean their house or run errands during the last few weeks of pregnancy. One partner saved coupons for the expectant mother. The pregnant woman greatly appreciated this and said what she looked forward to most was having the partner bring over the coupons and talk with her.

● **Parenting library**—Establish a collection of quality parenting books, cassette tapes and videos. Encourage expectant parents to rent or borrow them.

● **Baby shower**—Give each expectant family a baby shower. Make it a family affair and hold it at church at a convenient time.

IN-DEPTH INFORMATION

The Job Description for a Prenatal Partner

A partner needs to be committed to regularly meeting with or visiting the expectant parent. Expect partners to:

● Pray daily for the family and the baby.

● Regularly call or write notes to the family.

● Regularly visit the family in the home to deliver parenting materials, see if the family needs extra help at home, encourage the family to attend childbirth and parenting classes.

● Meet with the family to set a date for the ministry shower.

● Develop a rapport with the family so that the family will notify the partner when labor begins. Pray during this time, notify others in the church about the impending birth and visit the family in the hospital soon after the birth.

● Visit the mother and child soon after they leave the hospital to help the family with any needs.

● For about three months after the birth, frequently visit the family in the home to offer encouragement and answer questions.

—V.A.—

WORKSHEET

The Prenatal Partner Agreement

If you wish to be a partner in our church's prenatal ministry, please agree to the following guidelines and sign your name.

1. I am a church member or in the process of becoming a member.
2. I support the church's ministry.
3. I will be faithful to my assigned expectant family.
4. I will live a Christian life.
5. I will attend all partners meetings and the training course.
6. I will regularly attend worship services.
7. I will keep my home life in order.
8. I will regularly visit my assigned family.
9. I will evaluate materials I take to the family.
10. I will notify the ministry leadership if I become aware of problems in my assigned family that require professional help.

I have read these guidelines and pledge to follow them to the best of my ability. I clearly understand that if I fail to follow them, I may be asked to relinquish my partnership role.

_____   _____
(Signature)   (Date)

—V.A.—

In addition to giving baby gifts, give parenting tips and scriptures to the family.

● **Childbirth classes**—Offer childbirth classes with a Christian emphasis. Publicize these classes so people from the community may attend. Contact your local hospital to arrange for a qualified childbirth instructor to lead the classes.

● **Parenting classes**—Give parenting classes at a convenient time for families. Have expectant families attend these classes so they can form a support group for each other. Videotape the classes and make them available to people who get pregnant when few others are pregnant.

● **Nursery tour**—Explain the nursery's purpose, standards and requirements. For example, our church requires all parents of nursery-age children to volunteer once every eight weeks to help in the nursery. This tour can help ease parents' fears about leaving their newborn in someone else's care.

● **Infant dedication or baptism**—If your congregation practices infant baptism, help prepare the family for the occasion. If your congregation doesn't practice infant baptism, help arrange a dedication for each baby. In this way, the church can join with the parents in committing to train each baby in the faith.

Ministry in Problem Pregnancies

Prenatal ministry can get difficult when an unwanted pregnancy occurs. The sooner you learn about these pregnancies, the sooner you can help the parent and the unborn child.

When the expectant mother isn't married, a lot of stress can occur. Families may condemn the mother—or reject the child. This is not the time to be judgmental. The expectant mother desperately needs to know both she—and her unborn child—are important.

We often help these mothers find a place to live. Some need jobs, and we help them find work. Since a father isn't around to support the expectant mother, the partner becomes extremely important. The partner provides a link to keep the single mother in church. And the partner becomes the significant, supportive person who the single parent needs so much.

Recruiting Volunteers

After your ministry has been going for a while, it will be easier to find volunteers since a lot of people who have benefited from the ministry will come back to help.

But until then, you can still find volunteers. We presented our ministry to the church and asked for volunteers. We prepared a handout explaining the kind of workers we needed and let people checkmark ways they'd like to help. For example, we asked for people who might want to become a ministry partner (see p. 111), bake cakes for baby showers, organize baby showers or develop a church parenting library. Interested volunteers placed their handouts in the offering plate. And after going through the applications, we contacted people to help.

The Children's Ministry Foundation

Over the years our church's prenatal ministry has developed into an extensive, significant ministry. But we started out small. You don't need to start a full-blown program. We just started with one partner meeting the needs of one expectant family.

That's all it takes to start. Just link up one expectant family with a support person in your church and go from there. You'll lay a vital foundation for your children's ministry. And the ministry is one that makes a lifelong impact on the church, the parents, the partners—and newborn children.

Notes
■ ■ ■ ■

[1]Thomas Verny, M.D., with John Kelly, *The Secret Life of the Unborn Child* (New York, Dell Publishing, 1981), 21.

[2]Ibid., 47-48.

[3]Ibid., 49.

[4]"Dances With Rodney," USA Today (March 6, 1991).

[5]Jeff Kleinhuizen, "Traditions Guard Hispanic Babies' Health" USA Today (February 4, 1991).

CHAPTER 11

GIVING YOUR NURSERY RHYME AND REASON

■ ■ ■ ■ ■ ■ ■ ■ ■ ■ ■ ■ ■ ■ ■

BY JEAN COZBY

G reta recently said the reason she and her family chose our church was the love and care the nursery workers gave her son when they first visited.

Each week, Greta's 1-year-old son Billy gave her the craft he had done in the nursery along with a note. The note explained what Billy had done and gave suggestions on how Greta could follow up the lesson at home.

The nursery provides an important ministry in a church. It should:

● give infants and toddlers a good foundation for the Christian faith.

● allow parents to be part of the church's ministry.

● encourage parents in raising their children at home.

Jesus set an excellent example for us in Matthew 19:14, which should be our philosophy in working with children. "Jesus said, 'Let the little children come to me, and do not hinder them, for the kingdom of heaven belongs to such as these.'"

Essentials of an Effective Nursery

A good nursery doesn't happen haphazardly. I've found five keys to making a nursery run well.

● **Cleanliness**—Regularly clean your nursery to lessen the possibility of a child picking up a cold or other illness at church. Since babies put everything in their mouths, clean all toys and surfaces with a mild disinfectant each time the room is used.

Wash all sheets, blankets and other washable items after each individual use. Put wax paper on changing tables to keep germs from spreading. Toss the wax paper after babies leave.

This will add up to a lot of laundry. But the job can be divided among volunteers who can take one or two loads home to wash.

Require volunteers to wear aprons since babies spit up and spill things. We also have our nursery workers remove their shoes. This eliminates the dirt adults track onto carpeted areas and protects little fingers and toes from dangerous heels.

● **Safety**—Require at least one person with CPR and first-aid training to be in the nursery whenever it is in use. Post emergency numbers such as your local hospital and poison-control office.

Also have parents fill out a form listing their child's allergies, his or her exact age, and snacks the child should or shouldn't have.

Also ask parents where they'll be during nursery hours and at what times. For example, a mom may say she's in an adult Sunday school class from 8:30 to 9:30 in room 221. She goes to the fellowship hall from 9:30 to 10:00. She'll be in worship from 10:00 to 11:00.

It may even be helpful to ask parents to explain where they usually sit in church since most people sit in the same place. That way if an emergency comes up, you'll find the parent with ease.

● **Supervision**—Provide a safe environment for babies by having adequate supervision. Parents will feel more comfortable leaving children in the nursery when their children receive individual attention. One parent stopped bringing her child to the nursery after she realized her baby hadn't been changed or fed at all one Sunday. The sole nursery worker was too swamped trying to meet the needs of 14 children.

Safe Nursery Checklist

Scrutinize your nursery from floor to ceiling. Use this checklist to help make it safer.

- ☐ Is a smoke detector installed? Are the batteries good?
- ☐ Are children protected from sharp corners? Tape foam strips on corners of counters and furniture.
- ☐ Do highchairs and swings have safety straps?
- ☐ Are cribs safe? According to the U.S. Consumer Product Safety Commission, safe cribs have sides that measure at least 26 inches from the top to the lowest mattress support position; spaces between the slats no more than $2\,3/8$ inches apart; end panels that don't have cut-out figures that a child's head could get trapped in; corner posts that extend no more than 0.59 inches (about $5/8$ inch) above end panels; and a mattress that fits snugly in the crib.
- ☐ Are all unused electrical outlets covered with safety caps?
- ☐ Do diaper pails have secure lids? Children have drowned by falling headfirst into diaper pails.
- ☐ Was a non-lead-base paint used to paint the walls?
- ☐ Is a fire extinguisher handy?
- ☐ Is the first-aid kit stocked?
- ☐ Does the toy chest have a secure lid? If it has a free-falling lid, remove it.
- ☐ Are furniture and shelves secure so kids can't pull them over?
- ☐ Have toys recently been machine-washed or disinfected with diluted bleach?
- ☐ Are old-style radiators shielded so kids don't fall against them and get burned?
- ☐ Are all garbage bags, cleaning supplies, diaper pins, lotions and diapers locked in a secure area?
- ☐ Have you checked nooks and crannies by getting on your hands and knees and cleaning the room thoroughly?
- ☐ Are phone numbers for the local poison-control center and hospital emergency room posted near an accessible phone?
- ☐ Do rugs have nonskid backings?

—J.R.—

I suggest you implement these child/volunteer ratios in your nursery:

- Infants: two children for every worker
- Creepers: three children for every worker
- Toddlers: four children for every worker
- 2-year-olds: five children for every worker

If possible, have enough adult volunteers to allow one volunteer to greet each child as he or she comes into the room. This person can make sure that the child's belongings are labeled and stored in an orderly way. And parents will feel more secure leaving their children.

● **Security**—The larger a church grows, the less likely it is that the nursery staff will know every parent and child. Develop a way to ensure a child won't be taken by a stranger or a parent who doesn't have custody. We give each parent a "claim check" to present to pick up the child.

● **Discipline**—Children in group situations need a discipline plan formulated for success. Whenever you discipline toddlers, let them know they're loved for who they are, not for how they act. "Nothing is as important to a child's feelings of self-worth as the knowledge that he is unequivocally loved by the people who are important in his life."[1] Make only one to three rules. The rule "Don't hurt anyone" covers a lot of situations that can arise.

Nursery Necessities

Obviously nurseries need cribs, toys, rocking chairs and colorful pictures on the wall. But it's easy to overlook other nursery essentials.

● **Restrooms**—You need restrooms near your nursery, especially since children at this age are being potty trained. Make sure you have proper potty-training seats and supplies to clean up accidents. Consider having one nursery worker help children go to the bathroom. And ask parents how they're doing potty training so you can use the techniques the parents are using.

● **Water**—Young children need to wash their hands after they play and before they eat. Water can warm baby bottles and be a lifesaver for spills. Adults also need to wash their hands after each

IN-DEPTH INFORMATION

Nursery Discipline

If a child in your nursery bites or hits another child, follow these steps immediately to ensure the incident doesn't happen again.

● Talk to the child. Tell the child how he or she hurt another child and that it's improper to do that. For example, say: Jason, you bit Suzie and hurt her. She is crying. I wouldn't let Suzie bite you, and I'm not going to let you hurt her either.

● Have one person watch the child for the rest of the session. It's okay for the child to know he or she is being watched. Be ready to remove the child if another incident occurs.

● Tell the child's parent. Explain what happened and how you dealt with it. Ask the parent to also talk with the child at home about what happened and explain why the behavior was unacceptable.

● If the child repeats the incident the following week, immediately call the parent out of the worship service or class to remove the child from the nursery. Explain to the parent that this is the next step in your discipline policy.

Also explain to the child what's happening. For example, say: Jason, your mom had to leave her Sunday school class to get you today because you hurt Suzie. It isn't good to hurt people. We really love you and want you in our nursery, but you can't come if you continue to hurt people.

diaper change to avoid spreading germs. Ideally your nursery should have a sink.

● **Carpet**—Rooms for infants need to be fully carpeted to keep down noise and provide a cushion for crawlers. For 2-year-olds, have a room that isn't completely carpeted since children will make a mess with food. Also, they like to ride toys with wheels. But have carpet squares for children who want to sit and play.

Laying a Spiritual Foundation

It's not too early to lay a spiritual foundation for children in the nursery. Start with the basic concept of Jesus' love. Teach that concept by having nursery workers act lovingly toward the children. You "cannot overemphasize the importance of conveying friendliness and unconditional acceptance where learning is the goal."[2]

Sing songs of Jesus' love while rocking babies. When you hug them, tell children that Jesus loves them. "Talking with and singing to babies positively influences their verbal skills."[3] And by providing a loving environment where you talk about God, children will associate positive, warm feelings with God when they're older.

Karen was skeptical when her 2-year-old son's nursery class was collecting money for a small orphanage in Mexico. Karen wondered if the children could comprehend the idea of children helping children. But her son Patrick came home talking about how babies needed milk and he wanted to take his money each Sunday so people could buy milk for the babies.

Although children in the nursery can't think globally, they can learn how to give and help others.

Staffing Your Church Nursery

Dependable volunteers make your nursery work. Some churches require parents who use the nursery to take turns staffing it once a month, once a quarter or for one month of the year.

Allison felt she needed to help out in the nursery since she had three children. She wanted her husband, Mark, to make the commitment with her. It took a while to convince him, but he finally gave in.

Mark tried hard to remain unaffected by the babies. He always took charge of the child who fussed the most. One Sunday when Danny cried himself to sleep with his head on Mark's shoulder, Mark realized why he was needed in the nursery.

Allison quit the nursery after her 13-week commitment and joined the choir. But Mark volunteers in the nursery for one quarter of every year.

Nursery workers become more effective the longer they serve. Volunteers need time and practice to learn how to care for children. In turn, children need time to get to know and trust the adults who care for them.

Michelle was almost 1 year old and had never been left with a babysitter before she came to church. She cried a lot the first few weeks, but Amy made a commitment to help Michelle adjust.

IN-DEPTH INFORMATION

Teenage Nursery Workers

Before letting teenagers work in your nursery, develop a teenage nursery worker policy. Consider these guidelines:
- The teenager's parent or guardian must give permission for the teenager to work in the nursery.
- Nursery duty must be an addition to, not a substitute for, Sunday school.
- Teenage nursery workers must be at least 13 years old.
- Teenagers must attend an orientation meeting and complete a babysitting skills class.

—J.C.—

Soon Michelle cried less, but made sure Amy was always in the room. Amy continued to let Michelle know she would be there for her. By the time Michelle could walk and graduate to the toddler class, Michelle felt comfortable enough with *her church* to make the move without tears.

Children's workers often struggle with whether teenagers should help in the nursery. Young people enjoy being with babies, but they usually don't have experience.

Teenagers work well if you train them. Teach teenagers how to pick up and hold a baby, how to change diapers, how to feed and burp a baby and what kind of activities work best with toddlers.

Some churches enroll teenagers in a class at a local hospital or an American Red Cross babysitting class to give them training they can use in the nursery—and as babysitters. What a great way to minister to children in the nursery—and to teenagers!

Terri was 13 when she began working with the 1-year-olds in the nursery. Terri took the nursery training class and was gradually given more responsibility supervising the children.

Before doing this, Terri had had trouble making friends. She didn't enjoy being with other teenagers in the church. But after working in the nursery awhile, Terri changed. She became more comfortable with herself and with other teenagers. Furthermore, the leadership skills Terri learned in the nursery gave her the impetus to help more children. When the church youth group announced it would do an outreach project with preschool children, Terri planned Bible lessons and crafts for the children.

Making Your Nursery a Success

Most importantly, if you do the following three things, your nursery ministry will flourish.

1. Pray. Pray for your nursery workers, your ministry and the children on a regular basis. Pray that the children will experience love and security in your nursery.

2. Show your appreciation. Give your nursery workers thank you notes, birthday cards, small gifts. If your budget allows, have an appreciation banquet to recognize your volunteers.

Judith often made simple but unique gifts for each of the people who worked with the babies. She gave them things such as potpourri she made from rose petals, a wooden spoon she decorated, or a decorated container full of blended spices for cider or tea.

3. Show babies and their parents how much you care. If their children are well cared for, they'll feel comfortable bringing their children to the nursery every Sunday. And children who feel loved in your nursery will love to come back for more!

Notes
■ ■ ■ ■

¹James M. Harris, Ph.D., *You and Your Child's Self-Esteem* (New York: Warner Books, 1989), 26.

²H. Stephen Glenn and Jane Nelsen, *Raising Self-Reliant Children in a Self-Indulgent World* (Rocklin, CA: Prima Publishing, 1989), 55.

³*How to Guide Preschoolers*, compiled by Jenell Strickland (Nashville, TN: Convention Press, 1982), 7.

CHAPTER 12

DISCOVERING THE WORLD WITH PRESCHOOLERS

■ ■ ■ ■ ■ ■ ■ ■ ■ ■ ■ ■ ■ ■ ■

BY MARY IRENE FLANAGAN, C.S.J.

P lant a tiny acorn and a mighty oak will grow—not instantly, but gradually. Preschoolers are like tiny acorns. When we look at these young children, we feel as uncertain about them as we do about acorns. We wonder: Will they grow in faith? Will they produce? What about their quality? We wonder if the seeds of the Christian life that we plant will someday flourish in the lives of our little ones.

As gardeners carefully prepare the soil to plant a seed, so too must we as preschool leaders. We're preparing deeply impressionable little children for a spiritual awakening. And our preparation means truly living God's Word with preschoolers and helping these young children experience the joy of being alive!

Understanding Preschoolers

Contemporary psychological research has stirred a lot of interest in early childhood development. According to researchers such as Jean Piaget,[1] Erik Erikson,[2] Lawrence Kohlberg[3] and Rhoda

CREATIVE IDEA

Getting to Know Your Preschoolers

Reading about early childhood development will help you understand this age group better, but you need to spend individual time with each child to get to know him or her.

Prearrange a 45-minute home visit. During this time, concentrate on getting to know the child. Go to the child's room. See the child's yard and play area. Meet the child's pets and stuffed animals. Find out what interests the child, and you'll be able to minister to him or her more effectively.

—M.F.—

Kellogg,[4] physical, emotional, intellectual, social and moral development follow an orderly, consistent, recognizable and predictable pattern.

According to Piaget, preschoolers are in the preoperational stage, which Mary Ellen Drushal, author of *On Tablets of Human Hearts* breaks into two stages: preconceptual and intuitive. During the preconceptual period, children age 2 to 4 are egocentric; they don't understand how another person feels. Two- to 4-year-olds classify objects by a single characteristic, meaning a rose is a rose; a daisy is a daisy. However, children don't understand both are flowers.

Around age 4, children reach the intuitive period. At this stage children are still egocentric, but their intellectual capacity greatly expands. Children can use numbers (although they can't explain why), and they can classify things into groups. For example, chil-

CREATIVE IDEA

Photogenic Walls

Help young children "see" how they're important people in God's eyes. Ask parents to each bring a picture of their child. (Or you can have an instant-print camera ready and take pictures of children as they arrive.)

Label each picture with the child's name so parents and teachers can more easily learn all the children's names. Put children's pictures in the middle of a flower shape under the heading "Watch All God's Children Grow." Then in the lesson, refer to the pictures, explaining that God loves each child.

—L.B.—

dren now understand that both a rose and a daisy are flowers.[5]

As preschoolers begin making these connections, they also begin forming a foundation for their faith. "The first seven years [of life] constitute the period for laying the foundations of religion," says R. S. Lee, the author of *Your Growing Children and Religion.* "This is the most important period in the whole of a person's life in determining his later religious attitudes."[6]

How to Give Preschoolers a Spiritual Foundation

What are the Christian education needs of preschool children? What can they understand and do? This is the time to lay a foundation.

The goal of your preschool ministry shouldn't be to "give" young children religion. Preschoolers aren't developmentally ready for formal instruction in faith. They can't interpret scripture, understand deep theological concepts or participate meaningfully in the religious practices of adults. Preschool programs that assume young children are ready for these things can do a great disservice.

Rather, the goal of preschool programs should be to provide experiences that will encourage children to eventually develop a mature appreciation of the faith.

Thus, the top priority in a preschool program should be to provide a healthy, loving family environment. Such a program will reinforce the young child's sense of trust and independence. It will recognize the child's needs for self-awareness, self-confidence, self-expression and self-appreciation. It will provide a structure that successfully challenges the child's developing initiative and inventiveness. It will speak of God, the creator, who loves all things he has made. It will speak of the glorious Christmas gift God sent us—Jesus.

If children feel valued and accepted in your class, they'll want to return to experience more of these feelings. Eventually they'll want to learn about the source of these feelings. This becomes the foundation on which more mature faith understanding can be built.

WORKSHEET

Evaluating Your Preschool Program

To set up a preschool program at your church or to evaluate the effectiveness of your current program, answer the following questions.

Questions	Yes	No
1. Are your program's themes expressed in concrete ways children can understand and relate to?	☐	☐
2. Does your program avoid theological concepts and training that young children can't understand?	☐	☐
3. Does your program promote creativity by encouraging each child's self-expression?	☐	☐
4. Does your program avoid pre-drawn art, which suggests comparisons and standards beyond the child's ability?	☐	☐
5. Does your program respect the children's physical capabilities by not asking them to perform tasks beyond their level of physical development?	☐	☐
6. Does your program affirm self-worth by showing you accept and value each child's creative work?	☐	☐
7. Does your program provide creative activities that children can do on their own without an adult's direct intervention?	☐	☐
8. Does your program encourage parents to participate on a regular basis?	☐	☐
9. Does your program encourage parents to extend each lesson theme by giving parents additional resources for the home?	☐	☐

If you answered yes to each of the nine questions above, your program is educationally, psychologically and theologically sound. It will provide an environment that encourages later faith development in each of your preschoolers.

—M.F.—

CREATIVE IDEA

A Prayer Preschoolers Can See

Since preschoolers are visual and concrete, make prayer something they can see. Have each child cover a box or a plastic 2-liter soft drink bottle with colorful magazine pictures of things that are important to them. For example, a 4-year-old may paste pictures of a dog, a family, carrots, the sun and a toy on the box.

After the children finish their prayer containers, have one child pass around his or her container. Have children each take turns holding the container and praising or thanking God for one thing pictured on the box.

—M.F.—

Making God Real to Preschoolers

So how do we lead young children to discover a loving God?

The primary goal in preschool is to awaken children's friendly relationship with God. Later on, the child can more easily come to know God in the person of Jesus and in the Holy Spirit.

Because preschool children are self-centered, plan lessons that encourage young children to love themselves. Before children can love others, they must first love themselves.

But all your lessons shouldn't be geared for the self-centered nature of preschoolers. At this age, children are beginning to reach out to others. They need to experience lessons on family, friends and community that encourage them to love others. If 3- to 5-year-olds don't love people they can see, how can we expect them to love God, who they can't see?

Young children, by nature, live in a world where there's a fine line between fantasy and reality. Therefore, ground lessons in the concrete by dealing with the child's world. Help children see that sand, dirt, plants and animals are gifts from God.

For preschool children, their faith experience is based on life experiences. God's revelation occurs in the world of bugs and hugs. However, children need to learn to interpret these works of God—which is where you fit in.

The child's world is one of discovery. So when a 4-year-old discovers ants, share in the excitement. Explain that God made the ants. By sharing in the discovery and wonder with a child, we begin to lay the foundation for faith. It's in that quiet moment of wonder—when a little one says "wow!"—that a child's prayer life begins. Prayer should be fostered as natural and spontaneous rather than forced in memorizing formal, traditional prayers.

As preschoolers grow and develop, their first images of God come from their experiences with their parents. Preschoolers who have loving, caring parents will understand that God is loving and caring. Conversely, children living in difficult home situations may have trouble seeing God as loving. But that doesn't mean you should give up on these kids. Your loving relationship with them will show children that God truly loves them.

Making Religious Holidays Meaningful

Three- to 5-year-olds love holidays! And so do adults. But when we celebrate holidays—especially Christian holidays—we need to be careful what we emphasize. At Christmas, giving minute details of Jesus' birth isn't helpful. Since young children slip in and out of a fantasy world, they become confused by too much detail. Children will understand these concepts when they're older. For example, a 4-year-old will not understand the virgin birth. A child may end up thinking Mary had two husbands—Joseph and God!

Instead, emphasize the part of the Christmas story preschoolers will understand. Say God loves us so much that he gave us a great gift: his own son, Jesus. Talk about how happy Mary, his mother, was and how she loved and cared for Jesus.

In preparing Christmas celebrations, do learning experiences that let children experience the joy and happiness of this season. Explain that the holiday is a birthday celebration for someone special: Jesus. And you can give children the experience of anticipating a great birthday party, giving gifts and having fun.

Easter is the high point of the Christian calendar, but it's a tough holiday for young children to understand. They do not know what sin is, much less understand humanity's need for redemption. To speak of Jesus' death for our wrongdoing can evoke inappropriate guilt in a preschooler. To dwell on Jesus' suffering is pointless with a child this age.

What if children ask about the crucifix in the church or a Bible illustration that depicts Jesus' death? Answer such questions honestly and simply. Explain that some leaders were jealous of Jesus and told lies about him. He was punished because of what they said, even though he had done nothing wrong. He died, but our loving God gave him new life.

As you plan an Easter lesson, focus on springtime signs of new life. Later, as children mature in faith, these signs will easily become symbols of Jesus' resurrection. Dye and hunt for eggs; discover that they are the secret home of chicks who peck their way from darkness to light. See, touch and smell lifeless-looking flower bulbs and the glorious lilies that emerge from them. Pretend to be caterpillars that spin cocoons then emerge as butterflies. Bring a new baby to class and discuss the children's feelings about new brothers and sisters at home.

Rejoice together in the springtime wonder of God's world. Make Easter memories together. These are the seeds that later flower into a full life of faith.

Learning by Experience

Preschoolers' lives are grounded in the world of here and now. They learn by doing, smelling, tasting, feeling, hearing, seeing. They don't have a sense of history or the ability to understand the past. Therefore we should concentrate on the concrete values presented in scripture that preschoolers can understand. They can understand the loving care of God, loving one another and praising and thanking God. They can understand these concepts as long as we give them ways to experience them.

Preschoolers should participate in all classroom activities. And because young children learn by experience, encourage them to taste, hear, feel, smell and see what you're teaching in your class.

To promote young children's creativity, encourage them to participate, explore, imagine and express themselves. It is in concrete ways, along with a joy-filled atmosphere and a loving teacher, that a meaningful Christian experience can touch the lives of preschool children.

Notes
■ ■ ■ ■

[1]Jean Piaget and Barbel Inhelder, *The Psychology of the Child* (New York: Basic Books, 1969).

[2]Erik H. Erikson, *The Life Cycle Completed: A Review* (New York: Norton, 1982).

[3]Lawrence Kohlberg, "The Developmental Approach to Moral Education," edited by C. Beck, B. Crittenden and E. Sullivan *Moral Education: Interdisciplinary Approaches* (Toronto: Toronto Press, 1970).

[4]Rhoda Kellogg, *The Psychology of Children's Art* (New York: CRM, Inc., 1967).

[5]Mary Ellen Drushal, *On Tablets of Human Hearts* (Grand Rapids, MI: Zondervan, 1991) 54-55.

[6]Mary Irene Flanagan, *Preschool Handbook* (New York: Harper & Row, 1990), 6.

CHAPTER 13

THE EXCITING WORLD OF K-3

■ ■ ■ ■ ■ ■ ■ ■ ■ ■ ■ ■ ■ ■ ■

BY VINCE ISNER

I once asked a group of 5-, 6- and 7-year-olds where they thought God lived. A kindergartner responded first: "I know! I know! God lives in the clouds, 'cause I can hear him when he snores."

"That's crazy," chimed in a savvy second-grader. "He can't live there. He's too heavy. He'd fall through the clouds and splat all over everything!"

If you're looking for a clue about how best to understand children ages 5 through 8, just listen to their conversations. You're apt to find everything from God to Godzilla, and therein lies both the joy and the challenge of working with children in this age group.

Children experience a remarkable number of changes in these four crucial years, which makes it tough to group these children together in any one activity. But they do share a lot in common. Let's look at what makes these kids tick.

Their Bodies

Children are filled to the brim with energy! Most people know this. Yet many of the programs we plan for kids in grades K-3 have all the excitement of a final exam. Children need to move, to use their bodies to discover and experience the world around them. Remember this and you'll turn your good ideas into great ones!

For example, a Sunday school class recently learned how their denomination helped a small village in Sumatra to install a water pipeline. To dramatize what life in the village was like before the pipeline, the teacher took all the children outside to a nearby creek, where the children filled buckets of water, placed them on balancing poles, and carried them to the end of an adjacent field. When the children arrived, hot, tired and sore, they *knew* from experience how much a pipeline meant to a tiny village half a world away.

Children do need quiet time too. So much of children's high-tech world consists of computerized beeps and electronic explosions, of high-pressure commercials and sugarcoated come-ons. One of the best lessons we can teach children is the value of silence.

Structured quiet time can be just as engaging as physical activity when you do it intentionally. So just as you plan your physical activities, structure time for children to reflect, think and "listen to the silence." Silence will make the active times more meaningful because children will have taken time to process what their activities mean.

Their Minds

Before children reach the age of 6, they've made a lot of progress intellectually. Those first years, from birth through about age 5, have been referred to by children's expert Selma Fraiberg as "magic years."[1] This isn't because their world is full of wondrous, magical, ethereal images; it is because of their belief that their thoughts and actions cause events to magically occur. At age 3, a child may believe an angry wish might actually come true and hurt a loved one. Children at this age may also confuse cause and effect, like the little boy who once told me that trees are like giant

fans that make the wind blow.

All this is natural and necessary, according to Swiss child-development expert Jean Piaget. But by the time children are 5 or 6, most children begin to emerge from this "neighborhood of make-believe" to enter a more concrete world. They begin to look for things that are solid and dependable.

Piaget appropriately calls this stage the period of concrete operations. During this stage children look for laws and rules. They want to know what is and what isn't. Is Santa Claus for real or is he a hoax? Is it or is it not okay to swear even if they hear their dads swear? For the most part children at this age look for black-and-white answers. Things are either right or wrong. Up or down. Never in between.

I remember vividly when I was 8 years old. My pediatrician put me on a strict, bland diet for a stomach disorder. After one month both my parents and the doctors were amazed at how well I was able to adhere to the diet. "Incredible," they said. "How can an 8-year-old pass up soft drinks, french fries, and pizza and survive on Cream of Wheat, dry toast and Jell-O?"

It wasn't difficult for my little black-and-white-thinking mind to accept the diet. The doctor had made it clear what I needed to do to get well. I had to eat Cream of Wheat, dry toast and Jell-O. Why would I eat anything else?

While children at this age don't always see everything quite this concretely, Piaget says they tend to look for categories in which to pigeonhole new information. Children at this stage can reverse their thoughts; that is, they can retrace steps and think sequentially to some degree.

Just listen to the questions children ask at this age. The questions often center around this sorting process. For example, children at this age will ask questions such as: Did it really rain for 40 days and nights? Does God answer prayer? If so, why didn't God answer my prayer to get an A on my math test?

The tough part, though, is that while kids at this age think in black-and-white, the world isn't black-and-white. And one of the most helpful things you can do for children at this age is to gently teach them to find comfort in the gray areas of life. Explain that answers may not be the same for everyone. And be honest when they ask questions you don't have answers for. Children need to understand that some questions don't have answers.

Their Senses

Children learn through their senses. Dr. John H. Westerhoff, professor at Duke Divinity School and author of *Will Our Children Have Faith?* told me recently, "Remember that religion was first danced before it was believed." And that's so true for children at this age. A 6-year-old is less apt to remember what is *said* than what is *experienced.*

Even as adults, our faith has been largely experiential. Sure, we've pondered questions. But for the most part, the greatest expressions of our faith have been beyond our thoughts. We remember a hauntingly beautiful chorale. A breathtaking fresco. The birth of a child. The grandeur of a mountain range. A private moment in prayer.

Children in kindergarten through third grade know this language of expression perhaps better than anyone else. That's why it's crucial to give children opportunities to experience their faith.

Children should be able to experience faith in Sunday school, vacation Bible school, after-school church programs, weekly children's ministry programs and other children's ministry programs. Think for a moment. What do you remember most vividly about Sunday school? Do you remember the contents of the little leaflet you stuffed into your pocket every Sunday? Or do you remember a story your teacher told you in her sweetest storytelling voice?

Chances are, you best remember the moments. You remember the time your Sunday school class sang for the senior men's class and one of the old guys pulled you onto his lap and told you how special you were. You remember the smell of his Old Spice and the warmth of his large, wrinkled hands as he patted your cheek.

Or you remember how the teacher always let you turn the lights on or pass out the Bibles. Whatever you remember, I'm sure it has less to do with the lesson than with the way your teachers showed how they loved you. Children ages 5 through 8 are sensory beings.

So when you're planning your next program or lesson, drench

IN-DEPTH INFORMATION

Different Kids; Different Paces

Between the ages of 5 and 8, children learn at different paces. No two kindergartners are alike. And in some cases, one of your kindergartners may be as intellectually developed as one of your third-graders. Some kindergartners can read while some third-graders still struggle to read. But by fourth grade, most kids can finally read at the same level.

What might this mean for your ministry?

● Instead of dividing children by grades or ages, have multigrade classrooms. Divide children by their skills and abilities, not their ages. For example, group together all children who can read well (which may mean your group has 5- to 8-year-olds in it). Then group together children who are still sounding out letters.

● Have older children struggling with reading or writing tutor younger children who are also learning. That way all these children can practice, and it boosts the self-esteem of the older children.[2]

—J.R.—

it in a sensory experience! For example, why simply talk about the prophet Jeremiah when you could have the old guy over for a visit? Your pastor will be familiar enough with Jeremiah's attention-getting antics to do a great impression. All your pastor needs is a costume, and you can provide the audience.

Does your lesson mention Peter? With a couple of phone calls you can probably find a church member who has a rowboat and a fishing net. You could arrange for "Peter" to meet you at the lakeside or the riverside when he returns from fishing. If your church isn't near a lake or river, transform your fellowship hall or churchyard into a port. Bring real fish for children to see *and smell!* Have the adult acting as Peter recall the time Jesus asked him to become his disciple. After worship, cap the experience with a simple dinner of fish, bread and fruit.

Speaking of food, you can create a meaningful memory by baking bread as a class for an upcoming communion service. Imagine the aroma of hot bread filling the sanctuary! Or make goodies to take to a nursing home.

Try finger painting the creation story to music. Make a psalm into a music video. Take turns caring for a baby lamb as you study Jesus the good shepherd.

Use the talents and resources in your church. Hold a "cata-comb" class in the church's furnace room. Visit the church sanctuary while the organist practices. Even a quiet visit to the altar for prayer can be a memorable experience for children in kindergarten to third grade. Whatever your lesson, remember: The effort it takes to transform a lesson on paper into a memorable experience usually is small. And it's always worth it.

Their Spirits

Children ages 5 through 8 can be incredible givers. One of the surest ways to engage children is through service to others. Nothing drives home a lesson quite like living it.

I once asked TV host Art Linkletter what he believed to be one of the greatest changes in childhood in the last century. He replied: "Today children are not needed. In the not-too-distant past families were economic units. Children were needed to perform certain chores and to look out for the younger ones. Today they have nothing meaningful to do. That's one reason for their frustration as teenagers."

I agree. In our church we have a "Care Club." Its purpose is to create opportunities for service. Our kindergartners to third-graders do everything from picking up paper around the church to raising money for needy children overseas.

I've noticed kindergartners to third-graders are at their best when they serve others. They cooperate more. They're more motivated. And they display a more genuine spirit of warmth. Children's spirits can be nurtured in many ways, but one of the surest ways to teach character and commitment is to let them live it out in serving others.

Their World

Kindergartners to third-graders have less control over their lives in many key areas than in past generations. Although they enjoy more options for entertainment and pleasure, their days often begin early and are scheduled tightly before bedtime.

My neighbor is a good example. At 6:30 a.m., the children are awakened. They hurriedly bathe, dress and are ushered out the door to elementary school. The children usually gulp down toast or a pastry in the car and wash down their breakfast with a thermos of milk.

After school, the children board a van and are shuttled to day care where they remain until 5:30 or 6:00 p.m. After 11 long hours, their parents finally get them and play with them about 30 minutes before beginning the nightly bedtime routine.

Most adults might wonder what's wrong with this schedule since many of them live like this. But the schedule reflects extreme pressure on developing 5- to 8-year-olds whose world is rapidly changing.

As children move from preschool to elementary school, school (an outside clock) marks their time instead of their own internal clocks. Life becomes much more competitive. Most children get graded for the first time. They begin to judge their own abilities. And if they try hard and fail, children at this age may conclude they're not any good—and their self-esteem can plummet.[3]

Despite all the things that swirl about in our children's heads, some things remain unchanged. Children still need love. They still crave security. They want to know honest, sincere adults will invest themselves on their behalf.

Don't let a kindergartner's or third-grader's cool and sophisticated veneer fool you. These children feel joy, and they still long to trade their precocious moments for childlike behavior. Imagine what a treasure we can give when we help them each discover the sometimes-elusive gift of their own childhood!

Notes
■ ■ ■ ■

[1]Selma H. Fraiberg, *Magic Years* (New York: Scribner, 1981).

[2]Barbara Kantrowitz and Pat Wingert, "How Kids Learn," Newsweek (April 17, 1989), 50-56.

[3]Ibid.

CHAPTER 14

THE CHANGES AND CHALLENGES OF UPPER ELEMENTARY

■ ■ ■ ■ ■ ■ ■ ■ ■ ■ ■ ■ ■ ■

BY DAN WIARD

John is an A student and excellent athlete.

Kevin is overweight and hyperactive.

Lisa is an average student who loves physical activities, sports and boys. She's developing physically faster than other girls her age.

Dawn is shy and seldom talks when she's with a group.

Jason, nicknamed "hotrod," thinks of nothing but riding his bike.

Julie knows more four-letter words than the English dictionary.

And Timmy, who is skinny and wears glasses, is the object of many jokes.

These are fourth- to sixth-graders. They're physically active, self-conscious and moody. And many churches don't know what to do with them. Many of these older elementary kids don't want to be involved in the children's ministry program with "the younger children," yet they're too young to be with junior highers.

Physical Changes

Although they're at different stages of physical maturity, children in grades four to six are growing and constantly changing. Their personal appearance is beginning to be important to them. They're maturing sexually and have questions about their bodies. Most children now begin puberty between the ages of 9 and 14.[1]

Some girls at this age are beginning to develop breasts. Those with larger breasts may be the envy of all girls and get the attention of the boys. Or these girls may feel like outcasts, since they don't look like the other girls.

Fourth- to sixth-grade boys, like their female counterparts, are growing, but at a slower rate. They're physically more alike, since they experience less obvious changes. These changes, for both boys and girls, can contribute to a rivalry between the sexes. Teasing becomes common.

Because of these differences in physical maturity, children's ministers need to:

● Develop programs to intentionally build children's self-esteem. As children begin to think abstractly, they realize others are looking at them, and they become self-conscious.

● Do one-to-one ministry, helping children who have difficulty integrating their physical changes into their lives and self-identities.

● Help children understand changes in their bodies by offering a sex education program.

● Consider separating the sexes for games and recreation, since girls tend to be more awkward and clumsy because of their growth spurts.

Intellectual Changes

Older elementary children can make decisions and take initiative. They'll enthusiastically devote a lot of time (even up to an hour or two) to activities they're interested in. Yet if something's boring to them, they'll start wiggling within a few minutes.

Their reading and writing skills are maturing, supporting their new ability to think abstractly and reason deductively. They're aware that adults aren't always "right," so they sometimes challenge adult thinking. As children's workers, we need to recognize our vulnerability and respect children's answers. Sometimes they may be correct!

Fourth- to sixth-graders can question and evaluate different points of view. They can make personal decisions based on religious ideals, and can express their beliefs in writing. In most cases, the meaning they find in stories is more "felt" than "understood."

Unlike younger children, upper-elementary children become more interested in the church and Christian heritage. These children can understand how the Bible came into being and the difference between the Old and New Testaments. They can find Bible books, chapters, and verses as well as use indexes and cross-references. Dictionaries, concordances and maps can be used successfully with this age group.

Most significantly for faith, older elementary children begin to think abstractly, rather than having to identify each concept with one object in their experience. "God no longer needs to be thought of in human form; love is a feeling, not a gift from Grandmother, and sorrow is an emotion, not the tears themselves. It is only at this stage that children can begin to understand the doctrines of the church or begin to cautiously express their own faith statements," writes Dorothy Jean Furnish in her book *Experiencing the Bible With Children.*[2]

In light of these intellectual characteristics, we can:

● Begin discussing in more specific terms what it means to be a Christian. We can begin helping children find meaning in stories and seeking to apply truths to their own experiences.

● Challenge children intellectually as well as physically. Let the children be reporters and write a newspaper. Play games that require thinking as well as physical activity, such as backward baseball. (Kids play baseball but do everything backward. The person hitting the ball must run to third base instead of first.)

● Design lessons that will interest children. Vary teaching activities. In a Bible lesson studying leaven, have children make two pizzas, one with yeast in the dough, the other without. Use learning centers, storytelling, puppets and crafts. See chapter 9 for more about creative presentations.

Other Changes

Being part of the "group" is a priority for 9- to 12-year-olds. They often bow to peer pressure rather than stand up for what they believe. Because of this, involve children in planning programs and lessons. Provide enough information to guide them in making "life" decisions based on what they believe. Encourage them not to always give in. Children need to learn to work together and still express their individuality.

At this age, children are moody and can easily become frustrated with themselves. They often compare themselves to their peers, and many feel they fail miserably. That's why we need to give them ownership in decisions and allow them to perform difficult tasks that make them feel useful.

For more information about the developmental characteristics of children in grades four to six, see the developmental chart in the appendix on page 218.

Sixth-Graders: Where Do They Fit?

At times, churches find themselves in a quandary about which group to put the sixth-graders in. Many of these kids are ready to move on and get away from the "immature" fourth-graders. Yet these same kids are apprehensive about being with eighth-graders.

How do you decide where children in the sixth grade fit? Consider these questions as a starting point to explore creative ways to handle sixth-graders in your church:

● How are schools set up in your area? It's simplest to follow the groupings the schools use, and it can avoid confusion and help carry friendships between church and school.

● Where do sixth-graders most closely fit? Are they more comfortable with the younger or older kids? And if you think they don't fit anywhere, consider having a group of just sixth-graders.

● What size children's program do you want? Would you rather have a large group that includes a wide range of ages? Or do you prefer small, specific groups?

● Where do the children want to be? What about the other children who will be affected by the sixth-graders' desires?

● What are the maturity levels of your sixth-graders?

Once you find a solution to the dilemma, be flexible. See if the solution works. If not, change it. And remember: What you decided this year for your sixth-graders can be different next year.

The Best Issues to Study With This Age Group

When children were younger, teaching them seemed a lot easier. We could pull out a Bible story, such as Noah's ark, and the children seemed to enjoy learning it.

But as children begin thinking abstractly and making connections with their own lives, this approach becomes much less effective. Instead of starting with the Bible and making it apply to children's lives, we need to deal with issues kids face and use the Bible to help children respond to those issues.

These kids have a lot of concerns. For example, Johnny steals. Rachel is scared her mom will die like her dad did. Jimmy gets

IN-DEPTH INFORMATION

Fifth- and Sixth-Graders' Top Worries

What do fifth- and sixth-graders worry about? Search Institute surveyed more than 3,000 fifth- and sixth-graders to find out. The numbers represent the percentage of kids who say they worry very much or quite a bit about the item.

Worry	Fifth-Graders	Sixth-Graders
My school performance	54%	54%
Hunger and poverty in the United States	52%	41%
That one of my parents might die	50%	48%
How well other kids like me	45%	46%
Violence in the United States	43%	37%
How my friends treat me	42%	43%
My looks	42%	48%
That I might lose my best friend	40%	35%
Drugs and drinking around me	40%	38%
That I might not get a good job[3]	31%	28%

—J.R.—

straight A's, but cheats. Ten-year-old Sharon, who looks like she's 14, is being "courted" by an eighth-grade boy.

These children are going to learn about life from their peers, parents, trial and error, or from *us in the church*. So why not help these kids deal with the issues facing them while showing them ways to handle those issues in a Christian manner?

For example: June's classmates are cheating on tests. Everyone is doing it, and June didn't study for the test. Does she cheat, or does she just do the best she can even if it means a bad grade? Let children openly explore issues such as this. Have them open their Bibles to learn how God might want them to respond. Then let them discuss the issues and problems.

Yes, children can learn by starting with a Bible story. But if we start with the 20th century—with computers, music and television— we may reach them more easily. To be successful, a program for fourth- to sixth-graders must meet children's needs.

How Do We Keep Them Coming?

I've heard children's ministers say they have difficulty keeping fourth- to sixth-graders active in church programs. Community and school activities seem to be more of a priority for these kids than church.

A lot of children drop out of church programs because no one seems to notice they're not there. Follow up with children who miss two programs in a row. If you call children or send a note when they've missed a program, you let them know they're important.

Evaluate your program. Ask kids what they think. If they think it's boring, find out why. Ask what they'd like to do. Asking the kids to evaluate your ministry will expose how relevant—and effective—your program really is.

Interest Kids Now; They'll Be Back Later

People who work with fourth- to sixth-graders are finding that if they keep this age group interested in church, these kids will stick with church in the long term. When Scott Sutherland took a church job in Tennessee, he decided upper-elementary kids were

---

WORKSHEET

How Well Is Your Program Working?

Whether you have an established ministry for fourth- to sixth-graders or you're starting a new program, ask yourself these questions:

- How well do you know these children? What are their schedules? How far from church do they live?
- What is the purpose of a ministry to fourth- to sixth-graders? What do you hope to accomplish?
- How involved are the parents? Do they know what the children are doing in your program? Do you involve parents as leaders? Do you send frequent personal notes and newsletters?
- How creative is your program? Does it offer a variety of activities? Are children interested in them, or are kids bored?
- How involved are the children in your ministry? Do you use active learning? Do children help with planning activities?

—D.W.—

---

important. "I told the committee that hired me I would focus on the fourth- through sixth-grade age group," he says.

"When we promote this year, the junior high group will double. And in three years, the high school group will be very large. We're bonding young people to the church before they're bonded to other activities, such as band, baseball and football."[4]

To keep kids interested, designate special fun activities that only certain age groups can do. For example, Carl Jones has his sixth-graders meet with the middle school group. "The middle school group has a slumber party at my house at the start of every year," he says. "And the fifth-graders can't wait to get into sixth grade so they can go to the slumber party."[5]

Jones is creative. And by being so, he keeps his fourth- to sixth-graders coming.

You can too! Just design a ministry that fourth- to sixth-graders won't want to miss, and you'll have kids clamoring for more.

Notes

■ ■ ■ ■

[1]Kathleen Stassen Berger, *The Developing Person Through Childhood and Adolescence* (New York: Worth Publishing, 1986), 466.

[2]Dorothy Jean Furnish, *Experiencing the Bible With Children* (Nashville, TN: Abingdon, 1990), 60.

[3]Peter L. Benson, Dorothy Williams and Arthur Johnson, *The Quicksilver Years* (New York: Harper & Row, 1987), 64.

[4]Charity Lovelace and Rick Lawrence, "Starting an Elementary Ministry," GROUP Magazine (January 1989), 54-57.

[5]Ibid.

Part Four:
Children's Ministry Programs

CHAPTER 15

MEANINGFUL PROGRAMS FOR CHILDREN

■ ■ ■ ■ ■ ■ ■ ■ ■ ■ ■ ■ ■ ■ ■ ■

BY EARL RADFORD

I love a smorgasbord. Smorgasbords are fun because there's something for everyone. You can eat as much or as little as you want.

Such should be the case in a church's children's ministry program. It should offer enough programs to meet the needs of the children. But that doesn't mean you should start programs left and right. A juggler can only juggle so many items at a time. Balance is the key.

Before Starting a Program

In deciding what children's ministry programs to offer (and there are a lot to choose from) think through each program's purpose. Ask yourself these five questions:

1. How does this program promote Christian growth?
2. Does this program fit my children's ministry philosophy?
3. Does the program share the gospel?
4. Is the timing of the program right?
5. Is the program fun for both children and their parents?

Through research, we found there were a lot of mothers of preschoolers in our community who felt isolated. These mothers didn't know who they could talk to. Many first-time mothers felt unsure about such things as discipline, proper diet for their children and places to find bargains on children's clothes.

A group of mothers met and formed a ministry known as M.O.M.S., **M**aking **O**ur **M**othering **S**ignificant. Now more than 80 moms are involved. These moms meet biweekly and share ideas and needs. They have also reached out to the community, giving workshops and seminars.

Last year our preschool coordinator wanted to plan a week-long summer day camp for 3- to 5-year-olds. It would be similar to a vacation Bible school, only for preschoolers.

Before proceeding, we asked ourselves the five questions:

1. How does this program promote Christian growth? Three- to 5-year-olds would learn more about God through Bible lessons, stories and curriculum. And it would encourage children to apply these biblical lessons to their lives.

2. Does this program fit my children's ministry philosophy? Yes. I believe children's ministry should focus on letting children know God's love is unconditional and that church is a good place to be. Both of these emphases are consistent with this program.

3. Does the program share the gospel? Yes. The program would be Bible-based, and children would hear about God's love.

4. Is the timing of the program right? The day camp was slated for the last week of June. School would be out by that time, and the youth camp wouldn't interfere since it wasn't until mid-July.

5. Is the program fun for both children and their parents? Yes. Parents would be involved in the Friday-night awards dinner. Children would also be encouraged to bring their grandparents, aunts and uncles.

Starting New Programs

In his book, *Unleashing the Church*, Frank Tillapaugh suggests two criteria for starting new church ministries. His guidelines also fit with new children's programs.[1]

1. New ministries should be lay-initiated, not pastor-initiated.

In this way, the program has the congregation's support from the beginning.

2. There should be a group of people interested in the particular ministry. Otherwise, those starting the ministry will become quickly frustrated and burned out, trying to run the ministry alone, without support. I think at least 10 people or families who have the same desire and vision could start a new ministry.

Also keep in mind a new children's ministry program must line up with the church's overall goals of ministry as well as the church's philosophy of children's ministry. In developing a new program, follow this six-step process:

1. Evaluate the need. It makes little sense to create a ministry unless there's a need for it. What concerns do parents have? What needs are not being met with existing programs? Often a questionnaire circulated in the congregation or community can gather valuable information about needs. Talking with teachers, counselors and others who work with children can uncover additional information.

2. Establish a vision. What do you hope to accomplish? What are the ministry's goals? Only by establishing a clear vision can you keep it focused and effective. This vision also gives you a measuring stick to use in evaluation.

Write a brief mission statement that describes in simple, direct terms what the program will do. Use this mission statement in recruiting volunteers, choosing materials, promoting the program and evaluating the results.

3. Provide a budget and adequate facilities. Some programs require significant financial support from the congregation. Others have special space needs. Make sure these are in place before finally committing to the program.

4. Find qualified leaders. Many programs' success depends on quality leadership. Look for appropriate leaders. Chapter 3 suggests guidelines for recruiting and training volunteers.

5. Publicize and promote. Use creative publicity to attract people's interest and attention. For ideas, see page 157.

6. Evaluate. After three to six months, evaluate your program in light of your vision and mission statement. Is it doing what you had hoped? If not, what's wrong? How can it be improved? Or should the program be discontinued? These are tough, but important, questions.

Financially Supporting Your Programs

Jesus told a story about a man who was going to build a house. Jesus explained that the man must first prepare the plans and count the cost. Many times we venture into children's ministry programs only to find we don't have enough resources to complete the task and reach the goal.

Getting the church to financially support the children's ministry may be difficult at times. I've found these suggestions helpful.

● **Show the need.** Most churches don't have extra money lying around, waiting for someone to use it! They need to see that a new program would be a valuable ministry to support. Use data you gathered in planning the program to show the need for the program.

WORKSHEET

Program Planning

Each time you consider planning a program, use one of these planning sheets to clarify your needs.

Proposed program: _____

Goals of the program: _____

Mission statement: _____

_____

Description of the program: _____

_____

When the program will meet: _____

Space needed: _____

Supplies needed: _____

Volunteer(s) needed: _____

Number of children expected: _____

Budget needed: _____

—E.R.—

If possible, specify interest levels. For example, you might report that 20 families have said they would take advantage of an after-school program.

Explain how the resources you're requesting will be used—and why they are necessary to be effective. Show that this ministry would be a wise use of the church's resources.

● **Be specific.** When you go shopping for groceries, it always helps to have a specific list. The same is true when seeking a budget for a new program. The church is much more likely to "purchase" a ministry if it knows what it's buying!

Don't say: Well, we figure we might need $1,000 each year for this program. Instead, you might say: Providing snacks each week would cost $20, and we would need $10 of craft supplies each week. Be realistic, and show that you've done your homework.

● **Establish priorities.** Recognize the church's budget limitations. List the most important items at the top of your list, knowing that you might not get everything you'd like.

● **Create options.** Let the budget planners be part of the decision-making process by giving a variety of options for meeting your needs. If, for example, you need an overhead projector, gather information from several suppliers, and let the budget committee have input on which option to choose.

● **Accept others' decisions.** If you can't have the whole pie, then settle for a slice. You may not get everything you need, but you've made a step in the right direction.

Remember that the church doesn't need to fund every part of your ministry. Each January, I meet with the parents for an annual planning meeting. During this meeting I explain all the children's ministry events planned for the year and how much each one costs. That way parents aren't surprised by the costs, and they can choose which events they want for their children.

Scheduling Children's Ministry Programs

Children's programs will affect others within the church. That's why it's important to consult the church calendar before you choose times for a program. Ask the people involved too.

One time I scheduled a trip to Disneyland the same week my wife was due with our first child! Six months earlier it didn't seem like a conflict, but as the date approached I realized I had made a grave mistake. Fortunately, I found someone to take the children to Disneyland. I stayed home, and our son was born that day!

Since many working parents agonize over what to do with children who have a day off when they don't, you can schedule special events on school holidays such as Martin Luther King Day, Presidents' Day, Columbus Day, Veterans Day and the Friday after Thanksgiving. Also think about children's weeklong breaks such as spring break and Christmas week.

Planning a Special Event

Every once in a while it's important to plan a special event— even if you only have a few children in your church. These big events get children excited. And when children are excited, they bring their friends. Plus, big events can attract a lot of children from your community who may never otherwise come to your church.

The list of possible big days is almost endless. With some creative thinking you could make a big day out of any ordinary day of the week. Consider these ideas:

● **Bible Day**—Give $1 to every child who brings a Bible. Then have children play Bible games all day.

● **Super Bowl Sunday**—Have children dress up in their favorite football team's garb. Play football relays, watch the game (intermittently!) and eat soup on this Soup-er Bowl Sunday.

● **Bring-a-Friend Day**—Give prizes to each child and friend. Play games that require partners.

● **Circus Day**—Have children bring their pets to do tricks. Help kids learn clowning stunts and how to put on clown makeup.

● **Cheerleading Team Day**—Invite a high school cheerleading squad to demonstrate cheers and formations. Encourage the children to make up their own cheers.

● **God's World Day**—Celebrate God's creation with a field trip to a scenic area. Pick up litter in a park and talk about caring for God's world. Enjoy healthy, homemade snacks such as freshly squeezed juice and peanut butter sandwiches on whole-grain bread.

● **Bike Awareness Day**—Invite an expert to demonstrate bike safety. Some communities require children to register their bikes. If this is true in your community, invite someone to help children register. Have bicycle obstacle courses and other bicycle activities.

● **Chocolate Day**—Have chocolate ice cream, chocolate milk and a building contest using candy-bar wrappers.

● **Stuffed Animal Day**—Have children each bring their favorite stuffed animal. Have a stuffed animal awards party. Give ribbons to the largest, the smallest, the most nearly unique, the newest, the oldest.

The Special Event Countdown

To pull off a big event you need a plan. This is the countdown I use to get ready for one of these events:

● **Twelve weeks before the event**—Finalize all plans. Decide when you need to order any supplies, such as prizes, food or craft materials.

● **Ten weeks before the event**—Find volunteers to work on various projects in preparation for the event.

● **Seven to nine weeks before the event**—Do follow-up with volunteers. Make sure everyone is still committed to the event, and assess their progress on the project. Be sure all volunteers know how important it is that they be at the event.

● **Six weeks before the event**—Make banners and posters to publicize the event. Store the materials until you're ready to begin publicizing.

● **Five weeks before the event**—Begin your publicity campaign. Put up your posters. Make announcements from the pulpit. Tell other church committees about the event. Keep publicizing until the event.

● **Two weeks before the event**—Have volunteers divide the names of all the children on the Sunday school rolls to call and remind about the event.

● **One week before the event**—Review the entire event.

Music? Volunteers? Activities? Visitor forms? Materials? Parking? Snacks? Make sure everything is in place.

● **Five days before the event**—Have the senior pastor send a letter to each parent.

● **Three days before the event**—Call volunteers to make sure they're ready. Encourage them, offer your support and thank them for their work.

● **One day before the event**—Have a brief meeting with all volunteers.

● **The day of the event**—Have all volunteers arrive early enough to make last-minute preparations and to welcome children as they arrive.

Meaningful Programs

Whether you're considering a children's church, vacation Bible school, an after-school program, a parents class or a special event on a Saturday, each program needs careful planning and prayer. Only then will the programs be effective and successful.

So examine the needs of your children and their parents. See how you can best meet those needs and enhance your church's ministry. And you'll develop a children's ministry that's dynamite and life-changing!

Note
■ ■ ■ ■

[1]Frank R. Tillapaugh, *Unleashing the Church* (Ventura, CA: Gospel Light, 1982).

CHAPTER 16

SUNDAY SCHOOL FROM START TO FINISH

■ ■ ■ ■ ■ ■ ■ ■ ■ ■ ■ ■ ■ ■ ■ ■

BY BARBARA YOUNGER AND LISA FLINN

For most churches, Sunday school is the heart of children's ministry. In fact, this single hour may be the only significant contact a church has with its children.

Therefore, it's vital to develop effective and creative approaches that will make this hour have a great impact on children—now and throughout their lives. This chapter covers the basics of teaching Sunday school—from choosing curriculum to evaluating a lesson when it's finished.

Setting Up Classrooms

Set up child-friendly classrooms. In each class space, hang a bulletin board for messages, art, attendance charts and photographs. Mount bulletin boards and blackboards at the children's eye level so children can use them too. Have a cabinet, shelf or rolling caddy to hold supplies, books, tape or record player, and games.

If you meet in a larger room with other classes, you may have problems with noise. Consider meeting in a quiet hallway, an empty choir room or on the church lawn in warm weather.

For each age group, consider these classroom setups:

● **Babies**—Safety and comfort are the most important concerns with this age group. Examine cribs, seats, walkers, changing tables and toys for loose, missing or broken parts. Label cubbies, bins, or hooks that hold each baby's diaper bag and outerwear. Have comfortable rockers and other chairs for nursery workers. See chapter 11 for more in-depth information on nurseries.

● **Toddlers**—Toddlers delight in small tables, chairs and play kitchens. Set up the room for play, with enough toys to prevent confrontations between children. Some churches equip their toddler rooms with appliance boxes for children to crawl through.

● **Preschoolers**—Three- to 5-year-olds enjoy the same size and kind of furniture as toddlers. However, elementary-school furniture often works. Set up learning centers and play areas for children. For example, you might want to have a housekeeping corner, an area for children to dress up in different clothes, and an area with toy cars and trucks. Also have a table with nature items, a table with blocks and another table for Play-Doh.

● **Elementary-age children**—Have appropriately sized tables and chairs for children in grades 1-6, but don't set up the room with rows of chairs. Leave an open area for activities such as circle games and drama. Have a Bible resource center equipped with Bible activities and books. Set up tables for projects children can work on from week to week. Have a pen-pal center, a Bible treasure box and a Bible characters costume corner.

Choosing Curriculum and Resources

The key resource in your class will be curriculum. So before you choose, review the material from various publishers. Walk through several lessons as if you were actually teaching a group of children, noting how the activities would work in your classroom. Talk with others in your church about the options and priorities in selecting curricula.

Use the "Curriculum Evaluation Checklist" on pages 162-163 for your evaluation. Guidelines are also available in Iris V. Cully's book *Planning and Selecting Curriculum for Christian Education*[1]

WORKSHEET

Curriculum Evaluation Checklist

Use or adapt the following worksheet for choosing your Sunday school curriculum.

Overall Evaluation	Yes	No
Are objectives clearly stated, measurable and attainable?	☐	☐
Are lessons based on biblical truths? Are older children challenged to use their Bibles?	☐	☐
Are the theology and perspective compatible with your church and denomination?	☐	☐
Is the lesson presented in a manner that the children can relate to?	☐	☐
Will it challenge and interest them?	☐	☐
Does the curriculum address issues the children are dealing with?	☐	☐
Do activities and experiences affirm students and make them feel good about themselves?	☐	☐
Do activities relate to the theme of the session?	☐	☐
Are the activities fun for the children?	☐	☐
Do the activities help build relationships and create an atmosphere of togetherness?	☐	☐
Are the activities and methods new and creative?	☐	☐
Do the lessons involve the students in simulation games, field trips or other experiential learning activities?	☐	☐
Does the curriculum include appropriate worship and devotion ideas?	☐	☐
Are songs suggested? Do the suggestions reflect a variety of styles, tempos and cultures?	☐	☐
Are craft ideas matched with children's abilities and interests? Are materials included or readily available?	☐	☐
Does the curriculum provide ideas and time for active games?	☐	☐
Does the curriculum provide both small- and large-group activities?	☐	☐
Are visuals large, bright and sturdy? Do figures show action and emotion?	☐	☐

	Yes	No
Teachers Guide		
Is the guide easy to use?	☐	☐
Is required preparation appropriate?	☐	☐
Are suggestions given to help the teacher with special needs or problems?	☐	☐
Does the guide provide options to adapt the lesson to your specific situation?	☐	☐
Student Materials		
Are color and size appropriate for the age? Are the illustrations appropriate?	☐	☐
Do the materials include a variety of puzzles and activities?	☐	☐
Do the responses challenge students to make appropriate personal applications?	☐	☐
Do the language, content and length reflect the children's age and developmental needs?	☐	☐

—J.R.—

and *Harper's Encyclopedia of Religious Education.*[2]

In addition to curriculum, gather teaching essentials. Collecting creative teaching resources can be a challenge at first, but it's worth the time. Once you have the supplies, you can use many of them again and again. If you're on a tight budget, ask members of your congregation to donate supplies. Page 78 of chapter 7 lists craft supplies people can donate.

Gather basics such as right- and left-handed scissors, pencils, markers, crayons, glue, tape, staplers, a hole punch, and construction and writing paper. Also gather books, games, crafts, activities, posters, stickers and other objects that will enhance your teaching.

You may want to group items in topical kits. For example, a Noah's ark kit might include a picture book, a flannel-board story, a toy ark, a pattern for paper doves, and rainbow stickers.

Read the lesson plans at least a few days in advance to see if specific supplies such as glitter or straws are needed. Some leaders read through the entire year's curriculum (or at least a quarter's) and order supplies all at once.

Using Creative Teaching Methods

The word "curriculum" customarily refers to the print materials used for teaching. But in a broader sense "curriculum," which comes from Latin and means "the course of one's life," also includes worship, service, fellowship and Bible study.[3] So in your teaching, consider other creative methods such as these:

● Match elementary-school children with older members of the congregation before the worship service. The young worshipers will enjoy the guidance and praise their "grandparents" offer. Grandparents will enjoy having new "grandchildren."

● Organize a monthly potluck supper for the toddler class. Have the toddlers' families take turns hosting the group. Hire a teenage babysitter to entertain the toddlers after the meal while the parents discuss jobs, marriage, toys and parenting styles.

● Invite guests to your classroom, such as the dentist who volunteered at a clinic in Haiti, the person who repairs stained glass windows or the teenager who learned to sail at church camp last summer. Survey the congregation to find people willing to share their stories.

● Field trips into God's world are insightful at any age. The fretful toddler who cries when dropped off at Sunday school may forget her fears while taking a walk to collect pretty leaves. The third-grade class may learn Psalm 23 while pretending to be shepherds in a field.[4]

● When attendance fluctuates during the holidays and summer, consider combining classes into one large class. For example, hold an Epiphany party. Have children read the story from Matthew, play a follow-the-star game, eat star-shaped cookies and sing "We Three Kings of Orient Are."

Preparing a Lesson

Before teaching a lesson, read the curriculum for the upcoming months. Too many teachers teach from week to week without understanding the scope of the curriculum. Later these teachers realize they could have tied lessons together with an ongoing craft project or a special room decor.

Most lesson plans are based on scripture. Read the passage carefully. Determine how the scripture relates to the objectives of the lesson. Ask yourself why children should learn about a certain topic such as the parable of the mustard seed. Ask your pastor for guidance in selecting resources and in interpreting difficult texts.

After you become familiar with the Bible lesson, consider how to present it. Incorporate crafts, music, drama, games and active learning. Part 2 of this book gives in-depth information about these elements.

If you choose to read a story directly from the Bible, for example, know the scripture well so you can read with expression. Eye contact says the story is important. Consider using illustrated picture books, which are available in most bookstores.

One trick in teaching children is planning enough activities to fit the allotted time. If you can, jot an estimated time next to each activity on your lesson plan so you can add up the minutes to see if the lesson seems to be about the right length. But even if you plan well, sometimes activities go much more quickly than you had expected. Consider having an "Extra Time Box" on hand with books, games and puzzles to fill extra minutes.

Finally, remember God is with you as you prepare your lesson. Record your prayer concerns in a journal or write a short prayer at the top of your lesson plan. Keep a photo of your class on your refrigerator and pray for your students as you reach for the milk. One teacher posted this prayer in her classroom: "Dear God, let the words of my mouth and the meditation of my heart be acceptable in your sight. Amen."

Teaching the Lesson

Teaching starts before the children show up. Arrive at church at least 15 minutes before your class begins. Organize your classroom and materials. Do you have enough chairs? Has another group rearranged the tables in a way that won't work for you? Has the tape player disappeared? Are your enticing storytelling props, craft supplies and snacks hidden? They can distract children during another part of the lesson.

Children won't arrive all at once. Have an activity ready as

IN-DEPTH INFORMATION

Teaching Age-Appropriate Activities

Teaching works best when you choose activities that fit the children's developmental stage. This chart gives an overview.

Age	Activities
12 to 18 months	**Art:** large crayons **Drama:** puppets, dress-up hats, animal-sound games **Music:** noisemakers, singing, clapping **Games:** Peek-a-Boo, Pat-a-Cake **Play:** shape sorters, soft-shape toys, rolling toys **Ratios:** two infants to one adult, four toddlers to one adult **Attentions Span:** can vary by second and by minute*
18 months to 3 years	**Art:** non-toxic paints, paper-plate masks, Play-Doh **Drama:** finger puppets, dress-up, imitating animals **Music:** clapping, rhythm instruments, group singing, recordings **Games:** circle games, leader games, Mother Goose games **Play:** housekeeping, push-pull toys, blocks, dolls **Ratios:** five children to one adult **Attention Span:** 1½ to three minutes*
3 to 5 years	**Art:** clay modeling, cutting, paper-bag puppets, collage **Drama:** masks and puppets, finger plays, flannel boards **Music:** songs with motions, recordings, rhythm instruments **Games:** movement games, circle games, guessing games **Play:** play sets, housekeeping, blocks, puzzles, dolls **Ratio:** eight children to one adult **Attention Span:** three to five minutes*

Age	Activities
5 to 9 years	**Art:** papier-maché, murals, clay projects **Drama:** skits, role-play **Music:** songs with motions, foreign language songs, instruments, choir **Games:** games that switch directions and rules, board games **Play:** housekeeping, play sets, craft sets, block sets **Ratio:** 10 children to one adult **Attention Span:** five to nine minutes*
9 to 12 years	**Art:** various paint mediums, clay sculpture, fabric banners **Drama:** plays, readings, clowning, pantomime **Music:** reading notes, instruments, singing in rounds **Games:** team games with more steps, individual skill games **Play:** collections, models, sports, challenging puzzles **Ratio:** maximum of 12 children to one adult **Attention Span:** nine to 12 minutes per task*

*Children may stick with an activity much longer, but a good rule of thumb is one minute for each year; for example, two minutes for a 2-year-old; eight minutes for an 8-year-old.

—B.Y. and L.F.—

soon as the early arrivers enter the classroom. An intriguing art center will help convince a reluctant preschooler to enter the classroom. Older children will enjoy a classroom scavenger hunt, a doodle mural or a clever word puzzle.

Greet your students warmly. If you're a new teacher, have nametags to help you learn names quickly. Make sure the children know your name and know each other.

If some children bring a distracting object from home, have them place the object in a treasure box or on a trinket shelf during the class.

Before you begin class, allow a few minutes for everyone to settle down. Some teachers use a bell to signal the start of the class. Others like to play a recording of a song. Whatever you

---

MONEY–SAVING TIP

Fantastic Flannel Boards

Flannel boards are an effective way to present scripture to young children. Instead of purchasing flannel boards, make one by covering heavy cardboard or an old game board with flannel. Design flannel-board characters out of inexpensive Pellon interfacing, which adheres nicely to flannel and is easily colored with markers.

—B.Y. and L.F.—

---

choose to do, make sure the way you start the class tells kids, "This is going to be fun."

Begin class with a creative, fun game or other activity that ties to the lesson. Use the activity to build interest and to help kids loosen up and begin to feel comfortable with you and with each other.

Children will often interrupt a story or presentation with a comment or question. Say: No the boy didn't have potato chips; he only had bread and fish in his basket. Then go on with the story.

As children learn to read, teach them about the Bible's unique format—how it's made up of different books and where the books are. Consider playing Bible games and doing scavenger hunts to help children learn to use the Bible.

For example, before you read the story about Zacchaeus, give the children a listening challenge: What kind of tree did Zacchaeus climb? This will help children pay attention and listen carefully. Or familiarize children with the Bible by having them raise their hands every time they hear the word "praise" in Psalm 148.

When moving from activity to activity, allow a few minutes' transition time. Give clear directions. And don't feel discouraged if some children don't participate in every activity. Adam may refuse to sing, or Maria may balk at putting her hands in finger paints.

Try to avoid these situations by giving kids choices. Say: You may write a poem about Jonah and the whale or paint a picture of them. If a child refuses to participate, encourage but don't insist. Just praise children for their efforts. Children learn best when they feel secure in trying new experiences.

If a project bombs completely, quickly move on to something else. Tell the class: I'm sorry, but this clay is just too moist to shape into animals. But if the class is really enjoying an activity, don't rush it. Cut something else short.

Children love snacks. Young children may expect a snack every week. Older children won't expect a snack each time, but they'll certainly enjoy having one. Coordinate snacks to Bible stories and verses. For example, consider serving animal crackers when learning about Noah's ark.

Ending a Class

Review at the end of class what you wanted to teach. Review reinforces the lesson and helps you determine if the children understood the material. Ask the children what they liked best and least about the lesson. Don't let their responses hurt your feelings; rather, use their feedback as a tool for evaluation.

Some teachers end class each week with the same activity such as a prayer or song. One teacher lights a candle and asks everyone to gather for a silent prayer. Another teacher has the children add an item such as a sticker, fabric shape, or magazine picture to a wall collage. Each item reflects, in some way, the week's lesson.

Occasionally send home a small present such as a pencil, button or magnet imprinted with a Christian message. Homemade modeling dough, a ribbon Bible bookmark, or a Band-Aid for the story of the good Samaritan are other ideas. But however you choose to end your class, say a personal goodbye to each child. Thank each child for coming to your class.

Evaluating Your Teaching

Once the class ends, teaching isn't over. At home, review the lesson. What went well? What didn't? Write notes on your lesson plan and make it a part of your teacher journal. Your notes will be invaluable to you in your teaching years to come.

Pray for the students who were absent. Write or call them. Some teachers have found a midweek contact helps ensure more consistent attendance. Occasionally send children in your class a

IN-DEPTH INFORMATION

Handling Behavior Problems

Below are some common behavior problems you may encounter in teaching children of different ages.

Age	Problem	Ways to Respond
Birth to 18 months	Fussing, crying	● Meet basic needs such as feeding or changing. ● Remove source of irritation. ● Comfort with singing or rocking. ● Assure with a hug, smile or kind words.
	Feeling hurt or frightened	● Remove the object, such as a scary jack-in-the-box. ● Redirect attention to new toys.
	Fighting	● Help kids share by dividing toys.
19 months to 3 years	Saying no	● Set simple rules. ● Be firm and even-tempered. ● Give choices. ● Redirect attention to a new toy or activity.
	Fighting, not sharing	● Take away objects in dispute or suggest ways to cooperate. ● Comfort with a hug or kind words.
4 to 5 years	Fighting, not sharing	● Help with taking turns. ● Suggest a different activity. ● Separate children.

Age	Problem	Ways to Respond
6 to 12 years	Disrupting lesson	● Repeat class rules. ● Appoint helpers. ● Reward good behavior. ● Make lessons more active. ● Remove child, if necessary.
	Reluctant attitudes	● Provide fun and interesting activities. ● Acknowledge children's preferences. ● Have midweek contacts, social get-togethers and class outings.

—B.Y. and L.F.—

postcard, give them a call or invite them to your home for a spaghetti dinner.

As you teach and keep your students in your thoughts and prayers, they'll become a blessing in your life. As you help them grow in faith, so will you.

Notes
■ ■ ■ ■

[1]Iris V. Cully, *Planning and Selecting Curriculum for Christian Education* (Valley Forge, PA: Judson Press, 1983), Appendix 1.

[2]*Harper's Encyclopedia of Religious Education* edited by Iris V. Cully and Kendig B. Cully (San Francisco: Harper & Row, 1990), 175.

[3]Ibid., 174.

[4]Lisa Flinn and Barbara Younger, *Food for Christian Thought: Thirty-five Programs for Church Gatherings* (Nashville, TN: Abingdon, 1991).

CHAPTER 17

INNOVATIVE CHILDREN'S CHURCH

■ ■ ■ ■ ■ ■ ■ ■ ■ ■ ■ ■ ■ ■ ■

BY RICK CHROMEY

Editor's note: Since churches are divided on how to include children in worship, this book includes this chapter on children's church and a chapter on including children in congregational worship (see chapter 18). Each offers a rationale and practical ideas.

C hildren's church is one of the church's most vital ministries. Does that statement surprise you?

For years I would have disagreed, but not now. Children's church is the major point of contact between the church and families. A solid children's church attracts more kids than a weekly children's program. It overshadows a Sunday school, because parents who come only to worship services drop their kids in children's church, and skip Sunday school. Children's church becomes the only program for many children who don't attend other church activities.

That's why I believe a local church needs a children's church.

Presently, 20 percent of the children I see weekly at our children's church don't regularly attend Sunday school. Forty percent have *never* attended a weekly children's program.

Does that mean our children's program has failed? No. Rather it illustrates the importance of providing something solid for the children *when they come!* For my children's ministry, that means making children's church the best children's program I can offer.

The Need for Children's Church

Some people contend that children should *always* be in congregational worship. In fact, I thought that way for many years. But I now believe this philosophy can stunt the spiritual growth of children.

Why? Because it's difficult for a church to provide a fulfilling worship experience for both children and adults. One group or the other will be stifled in its worship as a result.

To expect children to respond in worship like adults reveals a misunderstanding of children's development. Children naturally fidget. They play with pew pencils. They ask questions—out loud! They have trouble reading the hymns. I used to believe the hymn "Bringing in the Sheaves" was an ode to raking leaves for pulpit disposal! No one ever explained a "sheave" to me.

Let me add, however, that children do need to know how to *act* in a congregational worship service. They need to know when to listen, when to sing and when to pray. That's why a good children's church program will have children participate occasionally in congregational worship. On the first Sunday of every month, we dismiss kids for a "Family Sit-In" Sunday. We feel it's vital for children to see their parents (and other adults) worship.

Types of Children's Churches

Children's churches are as varied as fingerprints. Created in the image, theology and philosophy of the church, each children's church is unique. No two children's churches are exactly alike— nor should they be. However, most fall into four basic types:

● **Snack-and-game hour**—Known as "glorified babysitting," this type of children's church can be destructive. Essentially, this approach views the hour as a time for games, snacks and crafts.

Kids think congregational worship is like a funeral compared to the snack-and-game hour. Thus as children get older, they often see church as the "bad thing that took away their good time." Fortunately, few churches use this approach.

● **Mini-church**—At the opposite extreme is a formal, adult-like approach to children's church. This church has mini-sermons, hymn singing and offerings. The problem with this type of children's church is that it fails to let children worship differently from adults.

I tried such a children's church once, simulating the actual conditions of congregational worship—complete with bulletins, pews and doxologies. After several months, the kids stopped coming.

Why? Because I didn't fit the program with the audience: children! The "simulated" worship faltered because it tried to make children into miniature adults. But children are children, not adults.

● **Extended session**—Some children's churches are extensions of Sunday school. In other words, children get a two-hour Bible lesson with activities, study and sometimes a snack.

Extended sessions can do well, but they don't prepare a child for the congregational worship experience. When children "graduate" from this type of children's church, they go to the regular church service, but many soon drop out because the church's regular worship service bores them.

● **Children's worship**—Children's worship is designed especially for kids, and helps them understand what's happening in congregational worship. It builds a bridge for their eventual "graduation" to congregational worship.

Unlike the mini-church approach, children's worship doesn't try to mimic congregational worship. Instead, it provides appropriate activities and experiences for children. It balances worship and biblical instruction, using group-building activities, prayer and shorter worship experiences.

Four Pillars of a Children's Church

So what are the important ingredients of a children's church? I think there are four essential pillars:

● **Worship**—Appropriate worship sets the tone for the entire hour. A good worship time will balance the lively and the quiet, the spoken and the sung, the contemporary and the traditional.

One objective of including worship in children's church is to prepare children for congregational worship. Songs such as "Father Abraham" should be encouraged, but don't exclude hymns such as "Amazing Grace." Every Sunday, we carry out the 3-2-2 system: three "fun" children's songs, two praise or scripture songs and two hymns.

You can also use children's sing-along cassettes. Several are available, including a variety of hymns, contemporary praise and scripture memory songs.

● **Active participation**—Kids often get bored with church because they're asked to sit still for too long—which doesn't let them release all their energy. To prevent boredom, include active participation in songs, lessons and prayers. Have children be songleaders. Invite children each to sing solos, share a poem they wrote or read scripture.

● **Need-oriented programming**—A successful children's church will address the present needs of children. When the Persian Gulf War broke out, many children were concerned. So in children's church, our children wrote letters to the soldiers and then prayed, using a map of the Middle East that showed where the war was.

● **Bible-basis**—The Bible must be central to a children's church. But use the Bible creatively. Play "Hangman" and use phrases from the lesson to reinforce learning. Incorporate scripture memory. Use role-playing, art and creative writing to back up biblical stories. Avoid using competitive Bible games such as "Sword Drills," since they can alienate children from each other.

The Bible is a truly fascinating book to children! A popular video series with our children's church has been *Superbook*.[1] Each month we use *Superbook* to introduce a new story and new "word" for the month. Beginning with Adam, we march through the Old Testament and New Testament month by month, story by story. We've discovered matching an appropriate word with a Bible story helps children recall the stories later. For example, when we studied Adam and Eve, we emphasized the word "obey."

Elements of a Successful Children's Church

Most children's churches occur during the congregational worship. That means a typical children's church lasts from 60 to 90 minutes. We incorporate three essential elements every week:

● **Celebration (20-30 minutes)**—It's vital to get off on the right foot during children's church, and celebration is the key. Let children *discover God* through creative worship experiences. Include praise reports, praise songs, announcements and offerings.

● **Communication (30-50 minutes)**—The central portion of the program is designed to help kids *gain and apply knowledge.* Communication must be on the children's level and incorporate a variety of teaching methods, such as: video, object lessons, art, music, simulation games, creative writing, puppets, "crafts with a message" and drama.

● **Cultivation (10-20 minutes)**—Every children's church should include a "take-home" challenge. Have "Share-'n'-Care" times where children affirm each other and talk about how they'll show they care for someone during the week. Children should leave your children's church every week feeling good about their faith *and* themselves.

Organizing a Children's Church

The organization of a children's church depends upon your objectives and philosophy for children and worship. Consider these three possibilities:

● **"Split-service" children's church**—Many churches use this model. Children attend the congregational worship service until a selected time—usually before the sermon—and then leave for separate activities.

What's good about this model is that children participate in a congregational worship service every Sunday and learn the rituals of worship. It also attracts more children, especially visitors, since the approach has high visibility in the congregation. It's also

---

Child-Adult Ratios for Children's Church

When are there too many children in a children's church? I prefer the "20" guideline. When you get more than 20 kids, create a new group. For example, if you have 25 kids, and 10 are preschoolers and 15 are in K-5, I suggest you create a "wee worship" for the 10 preschoolers and a children's church for the older kids.

A church with 25 preschoolers and 45 kids in K-5 might divide into four children's churches: one for 2- and 3-year-olds, another for 4- and 5-year-olds, another for K-2, and one for grades 3-5.

You might even consider having a portion of the children's church together each week and then dividing into age groups. In our children's church, we have a song and offering time for all 2-year-olds through grade 5. Then we divide into three groups: one for 2- to 3-year-olds, another for 4- and 5-year-olds and another for kids in grades 1-5. When one of those groups reaches 20, we'll split again.

—R.C.—

---

easier to recruit leaders since they can at least attend part of the worship service.

But there are disadvantages. The disruption of children leaving the worship service can create confusion. Another disadvantage is children rarely experience an entire congregational worship, which may make their eventual "graduation" into the congregational worship experience more difficult.

● **Self-contained children's church**—I think this model is more effective than the split-church model. In this type of church, children are separated from the adults the entire hour, meeting elsewhere in the church.

The self-contained children's church can encourage spiritual growth in children. However, the danger with this format is children *never* experience congregational church until they're older. Often the stark differences between the children's church and the congregational worship service then turn children away.

For this model to be effective it must:

● Let children occasionally worship with the adults. Some children's churches do this once a month, some on only the fifth

Rate Your Children's Church

Answer these questions to see if your children's church is on track.

	Yes	No
1. Do children in your children's church worship with the adults at least once a quarter?	☐	☐
2. Has each child been involved in your children's church at least once in the past month?	☐	☐
3. Do your lessons each include a topic, activities and illustrations that interest children?	☐	☐
4. Are children excited about your children's church?	☐	☐
5. When children attend congregational services do you provide exercises that help kids listen?	☐	☐

Count the number of times you answered yes.

● If you said yes five times, congratulations! You're doing a great job.

● If you have three or four yes answers, you're doing well, but there's room to improve.

● If you answered yes twice or less, use the ideas from this chapter to build a stronger children's church.

—R.C.—

Sundays. Special holidays such as Christmas and Easter should also be times when children can worship with adults.

● Prepare children for congregational worship. Help kids understand the traditions and rituals of your worship service. Explain liturgies and hymns. Answer questions about issues such as communion.

● Develop children's talents for church. Children have a remarkable gift: they often don't recognize a lack of talent! For example, children enjoy singing, oblivious to the fact that many sing off-key. A successful children's church challenges children to express themselves, even if they don't have natural talent in a particular area.

● **The extended session**—Extended sessions work well with younger children, and many curriculum companies provide excellent resources for this format. However, using this format with elementary-school children may come back to haunt you later, since it doesn't introduce children to worship and begin preparing them for it. That's why I think extended sessions have only a limited place in children's ministry.

Measuring Your Success

I believe children's church proves its value when children show that they have learned how the church worships and about its worship traditions. One of the greatest joys of a children's church is watching children "graduate" to the congregational worship service and become active participants.

In the end, then, an effective children's church program has an important impact on all aspects of children's and youth ministries, since it develops in children the desire to and interest in worshiping God.

Note
■ ■ ■ ■

[1] *Superbook* (Wheaton, IL: Tyndale House).

CHAPTER 18

WORSHIP WITH THE WHOLE CHURCH

■ ■ ■ ■ ■ ■ ■ ■ ■ ■ ■ ■ ■ ■ ■ ■ ■

BY WES HAYSTEAD

Editor's note: Since churches are divided on how to include children in worship, this book includes this chapter on including children in congregational worship and a chapter on children's church (see chapter 17). Each offers a rationale and practical ideas.

What do children in your church gain from being in the congregational worship service?

At what age does your church expect children to sit with their parents during church?

How can you help children understand and participate meaningfully in your church's worship experiences?

How can you help parents make worship a positive family experience?

These are only a few questions every church needs to periodically explore to be effective in reaching children and their families. Though some of these questions may be difficult to answer, I believe families should worship together. Some of the benefits of including children in worship:

● Children feel a sense of belonging to the church family.

● Children get to know church leaders and members of the congregation.

● It brings family members together instead of separating them.

● Children learn how your church worships by observing parents and other adults.

● Children enjoy participating in meaningful worship experiences.

● Children learn more about God.

In advocating including children in congregational worship, I'm aware of the problems that can arise. Whenever you have children in congregational worship services, you'll have adjustments to make. These problems always stem from the differences between children and adults. Their ability to sit still is different. Their attention spans are different. And so are their vocabularies, interests and needs.

In most cases, children point out these differences. They daydream. They count ceiling tiles. They pester parents. And they play Peek-a-Boo with people sitting behind them.

Unfortunately, once children tune out what's happening, it's difficult to capture their attention and get them to participate in the service.

Although we can't erase the differences between children and adults, we can take specific steps to make worship meaningful for both children and adults.

The Challenges of Worship

How well does your church involve children in various aspects of your church's worship service? Let's look at each component individually.

● **Welcoming children to church**—Most churches help people feel welcome. Congenial people shake hands, smile and offer a friendly word. But these friendship rituals aren't always friendly to children.

Observe welcome times and see how often adults ignore the children. Some adults reach across the top of a child's head to shake hands with an adult. Or people may say things that make children feel uncomfortable such as: "My, aren't you a big boy now?" "You look just like your sister."

● **Congregational singing and special music**—Children's involvement in singing depends on what's being sung. Children rarely sing hymns that don't have repeating phrases or choruses. Churches that use an overhead projector to show the words of hymns sometimes make it difficult for children to participate by having everyone stand to sing. "How can I sing, Mom?" a little boy will ask. "The guy in front of me is blocking the words!"

Hymns, gospel songs and choruses also tend to use words and phrases a child doesn't understand. Some lyrics are highly symbolic, posing major hurdles for literally minded children to try to jump over.

● **Announcements**—Rarely are the announcements the high point of the service for people of any age. But does your church regularly have announcements for the children? If not, no wonder they don't pay attention.

● **Children's talk**—Congregations rate a children's talk as one of the most popular features of the service. But just because adults like it doesn't mean kids do. Evaluate whether the message is really concrete and the children really enjoy this part of the service.

● **Offering**—Even though they may not understand the significance of the offering, kids love passing the offering plate—especially if they get to put something in it. They also like it if the ushers smile at them when passing the plate.

● **Special observances (such as baptism and communion)**—Usually a child does heavy-duty daydreaming during these parts of the service. Although children like to watch people move and to look at objects such as water and bread, these observances usually last too long for a child—especially if the child isn't involved.

● **Scripture reading**—Many children enjoy trying to locate a passage in the Bible, but often the reading begins while they're still searching for the passage. While the passage may catch the child's attention, especially if it recounts a familiar story, most passages are full of unfamiliar words and thoughts.

● **Prayer**—Most children rank prayer as the most boring part of the service. The length of the prayer combined with the effort to keep eyes closed and head bowed make prayer an ordeal for children. The problem is compounded by the child knowing that

WORKSHEET

Evaluate Your Worship Service

Evaluate whether your congregational worship is child-friendly. Or better yet, survey each parent. How well do each of these aspects of your church worship involve children?

Worship Element	Very Well	Okay	Not Well
Welcoming to the worship service	☐	☐	☐
Congregational singing	☐	☐	☐
Announcements	☐	☐	☐
Scripture reading	☐	☐	☐
Children's sermon or talk	☐	☐	☐
Prayer	☐	☐	☐
Offering	☐	☐	☐
Special observances (such as communion, baptism)	☐	☐	☐
Special music	☐	☐	☐
Sermon	☐	☐	☐

—W.H.—

any noise made while the pastor prays will be immediately met by sharp parental disapproval.

● **Sermon**—All children quickly learn the skill of tuning out adult voices. And for a child, a 20-minute sermon is way too long.

A few months ago, our pastor preached on abortion, a topic my 11-year-old son and I had discussed just a few weeks earlier. I thought he'd be interested to hear what the pastor had to say.

On the way home, I asked him what he learned about abortion. My son looked at me with a blank stare and responded, "Abortion?"

"Sure," I said, "abortion. That's what the sermon was about."

"Oh, yeah," he replied. "I noticed that in the bulletin, but I wasn't paying any attention then."

"So, what were you doing?" I pursued.

"Thinking," he said.

Effective Ways to Include Children in Worship

To make worship worthwhile for children and adults, meet with the parents to give them ideas. These suggestions aren't guaranteed to make all the problems go away. But they're proven techniques that any parent can use in helping a child gain more from the worship service.

● Tell the child one reason you as a parent like to attend the worship service.

● Visit the restroom and drinking fountain before entering. This can avoid a host of problems within the next hour.

● Enter worship about five minutes before the service begins. Some parents mistakenly try to delay their arrival so they can slip in a little late and reduce the amount of time their children have to sit still. However, children don't feel comfortable coming in late when the action is already in progress. Arriving a few minutes early allows time to help the child feel as comfortable as possible.

● Greet the ushers and other worshipers sitting nearby, making sure to introduce these grown-ups to the child as personal friends.

● Look around for someone the child knows (other children, relatives or Sunday school teachers). Catch these people's attention and encourage the child to smile back. This helps children feel a sense of community as they see others they know worshiping together.

● Sit near the front. Children feel much more a part of something by being up close than by observing something at a distance. Sitting up front helps the child see who is speaking or singing. Sitting in front also helps speakers be more aware that children are in the congregation and should be given consideration. If children are considered part of the worshiping community, any "disturbance" at the front will be accepted as a natural part of the community of faith.

● If the order of service is printed in the bulletin, find at least one thing your child can do to prepare for it. For example, the child may locate the page of the first hymn to be sung. Consider giving your child a pencil or crayon to mark off each part of the service as it occurs.

CREATIVE IDEA

After-the-Service Talk Tips

Give parents these ideas to use with their children after the service. These talk tips will encourage children to pay more attention if they know their parents will talk about the worship service each Sunday.

● Ask each other questions about what went on in the service. Be prepared for the child to focus on things you may not feel were important.

● Tell something you learned or were reminded of that you feel is important for your life.

● Affirm the child for specific ways he or she participated and showed positive behavior.

—W.H.—

● Encourage the child to look and listen for something in the service to ask you a question about afterward.

● Share a hymnal with the child. One hand on the book and the other on the child's shoulder helps make congregation singing a family time even if the child doesn't understand what the song is about. If the child is a beginning reader, use your finger to point to the words on the page.

● Help the child locate any Bible passages to be read. Take time before or after church to help the child practice finding books, chapters and verses.

● Gently encourage the child to participate as much as possible. When the congregation stands, have the child stand also. If people are told to shake hands, shake the child's hand first then lead him or her to greet someone else.

● Have a small treat, such as Life Savers. Tell the child in advance that two times during the service you will give the treat to show the child is doing well. Make it clear that the child can't ask for the treat. Don't set too strict a standard for good behavior. Look for signs that the child is trying.

● Bring along activity or coloring books, drawing paper, pencils, crayons or felt markers. Let the child know the point in the service (such as during the sermon) that you'll let the child use these items quietly. These activities will keep kids interested in times when they are developmentally unable to concentrate on the congregational worship.

Planning a Meaningful Service

As a children's worker, meet regularly with the senior pastor to discuss ways to involve children in the worship service. Consider the following ideas to make the worship service more meaningful and enjoyable for children.

● Consider children's needs and interests when planning the service. You wouldn't expect a group of deaf people to sit through a service without the help of an interpreter. But few church leaders give consistent, conscious thought to the children scattered throughout their congregation.

● Have worship leaders periodically visit children's groups to talk about what goes on in worship. Children will listen better to pastors, music leaders, ushers and other leaders when they've met them up close. This will also help these leaders recognize the presence of children as part of the congregation.

A seminary intern, who for almost a year had been assisting the pastor in leading worship, came out of the first-grade classroom with a glazed look. For five minutes he had tried to explain the main thrust of the morning's worship service. After closing the door behind him, he said: "Wow! I'm glad that's over. I don't have a clue how to talk to those kids." The teacher's reply startled him: "That's too bad, 'cause those kids have been in every worship service you've led since you've been here."

● Train ushers and greeters in how to welcome children. Encourage them to stoop down and talk eye-to-eye with a preschooler. Explain to them that children will rarely initiate contact with an adult they don't know well. But children feel good when an adult says hello to them and calls them by name.

● Include at least one hymn or song that children can easily learn and sing. Choose hymns with repeating phrases or choruses. Even if the child misses a lot of the words, he or she can join in on the refrain.

● When addressing contemporary issues during prayers or the sermon, think about the concerns of children. For example, the phase "showing God's love at home, in your community and at work ..." can easily include children by adding "at school" and "on the playground." Instead of just referring to "men and women" also include "girls and boys" or "children."

● Provide a children's bulletin or worksheet for each child. Include questions about things that will happen in the service, what to look for in the scripture reading and some simple questions about the sermon. Then consider having some puzzles included that relate to the sermon's topic. Even if the child doesn't listen to the sermon, he or she can gain something by doing the puzzle in the children's bulletin.

● Actively involve children in your worship service. Have children read aloud short scripture passages, hand out bulletins, assist greeters in welcoming people, collect the offering (this is a great task for the whole family), hold up a sign or poster to help with an announcement, provide special music, place transparencies on the overhead projector or move a microphone when needed.

A sense of belonging doesn't grow automatically for children. But it does flourish when children know other people and feel loved and needed. Just because adults participate in a worship service doesn't mean a child shouldn't. After all, when did Samuel get his start?

CHAPTER 19

ADVENTURES IN VACATION BIBLE SCHOOL

■ ■ ■ ■ ■ ■ ■ ■ ■ ■ ■ ■ ■ ■ ■ ■

BY MITCHELL PICARD

Vacation Bible school is a great way to reach children and their families. But unfortunately too many churches are chucking vacation Bible school. Everyone is busy. The standard curricula don't always attract the kids. Volunteers seem non-existent. And these programs are a lot of work. But with a little creativity, vacation Bible school can become a vital part of your children's ministry.

Rethinking Vacation Bible School

Creativity involves more than just using new decorations or figuring out a new way to twist someone's arm to volunteer. Over the years VBS has drifted into a bad habit: too many churches try to run it as a weeklong Sunday school. We need to update this program so that it meets people's needs today. Things to consider:

● **When to have it**—So often we assume vacation Bible school must take place during one week of the summer during the day. But why?

Consider having a one-day program or a vacation Bible school for the entire family that meets in the evenings. And why have it only in the summer? What about other vacation times such as Christmas break and spring break?

We've found evenings work best because more adults can help. We also think early June or mid-August works best during the summer. July is a bad month because many kids either go to camp or are traveling with their families.

● **Why have it**—Think through the purpose of your vacation Bible school. One church decided to quit having the summer week-long program because the church had only five children and the other 50 children came from other churches. "These kids never come back to our church," said one church member, "so why have it?"

This kind of thinking is dangerous. Vacation Bible school attracts children from the community who might not otherwise come to your church. Is your purpose to help children grow spiritually? attract people from the community? provide a service to families?

Fifteen years ago a 5-year-old girl, who had never attended church before, came to our VBS. The program got her so excited about church that she faithfully rode the bus to church every Sunday, even though her parents didn't attend. Eventually her mother came to our church to see exactly what her daughter was doing. As a result, her whole family now attends church regularly.

● **Which ages to include**—Most vacation Bible schools are for elementary-age kids. We also run a VBS for preschool-age children. Some churches even have family vacation Bible schools where parents can learn bread making, how to fix a gourmet meal, how to manage family finances or how to become better parents while their children have their own VBS classes.

● **How to do it**—Ready-made vacation Bible school materials can be valuable and helpful. But think about whether the prepackaged materials really meet the needs of your kids and say what you want to say. Consider creating your own or adapting existing resources to fit the specific needs of your church. Think of your own themes and ideas and gather games, teaching techniques, crafts and other ideas from various sources.

CREATIVE IDEA

Encouraging Kids to Bring Their Friends

Give children each an award or points each time they attend and for each visitor they bring. We tally points at the end of our vacation Bible school and have an "awards store" filled with lots of items kids like (such as stickers, fast-food coupons and toys). Kids trade their points for whatever they can "afford." This plan motivates children to attend and bring their friends.

—M.P.—

10 Creative VBS Themes

I've developed a number of VBS themes that have attracted a lot of kids. So entice kids to vacation Bible school with these child-pleasing themes—or think of your own!

● **The Greatest Bible School on Earth**—Children enter a circus tent, complete with cutouts of animals, a trapeze, balloons, clowns and a circus wagon. Animal puppets sing gospel songs. A ringmaster announces Bible stories about the world's strongest man (Samson) and the world's best lion tamer (Daniel).

● **Sail the High Seas for Hidden Treasure**—Captain Hook and his zany pirates help children search all week for treasures. Kids hunt for pieces of a map that leads to a treasure. Serve lime sherbet and call it "frozen seaweed juice."

● **Terrific Time-Train Express**—The conductor, using puppets, drama skits and Bible characters, invites children to get aboard and travel back through the scriptures.

● **In the King's Court**—Kings and knights challenge kids to discuss the armor of God as the dragon attempts to capture each knight and take over the castle. Put marshmallows onto pretzel sticks and call them lances for the knights.

● **Found in Space**—When kids arrive, space people greet them and little green puppets sing from moon craters. Captain Share-the-Faith leads kids on a space journey to learn how important it is for them to follow God.

● **South of the Border**—Everything from piñatas to a Spanish villa sets the atmosphere for a "hot" place. Sheriff Saintly tells how to defeat the different bandits who try to take over the town.

● **The Magic Time Machine**—Children travel back through time in a magic time machine to learn about the special people and places in the Bible.

● **The Great Western Roundup**—Kids dress up like cowboys. They sit around the corral listening to Roy Roundup tell about Christ's travels in the desert and how he reacted to his problems. Have children round up their friends to come.

● **Fort Wilderness**—In a fort, children sit around a makeshift bonfire. They listen to scriptures that challenge them to place Jesus first in their lives as they travel through the wilderness of life.

● **Up, Up and Away**—Balloons, balloons and more balloons adorn your church. Children experience an incredible ride as their balloon captain takes them to areas of the world where missionaries go.

Vacation Bible School Ingredients

Once you put a lot of creativity into your vacation Bible school, make sure you're not throwing out some of the essential ingredients that you still need to have to make your vacation Bible school successful.

● **Publicity**—Design fliers, posters, buttons, bumper stickers—anything to get the word out about your program. Consider asking a child to design the publicity then go to a local print or copy shop to make fliers. Hang the posters around your church, and mail fliers to prospective families. Also ask church members to distribute posters and fliers to appropriate businesses and service organizations. Place ads in your local newspaper and with the local radio station. These ads aren't as expensive as you might think.

● **Decorations**—Design decorations to hang throughout the church. For example, if your vacation Bible school theme is "Kids in Space" hang stars and rockets made from aluminum foil throughout the church. Get the kids' attention with these decorations.

● **Registration**—This is the vital link between each child and the church. We have an information card for each child. We use this information for emergencies and for follow-up after the event.

Have parents fill out these cards when they bring their children the first day or mail the cards a week before your VBS starts for the child to bring on the first day.

● **Bible learning experiences**—Build creative learning experiences throughout the VBS experience. Tie the week's theme to various scripture passages. For example, if you used the theme "In the King's Court" (page 193), you could focus on Ephesians 6:10-20, which talks about the armor of God. This passage could be approached from many angles to help kids understand how their faith can make a difference in their lives.

Have kids learn about the Christian faith and about the Bible through creative games, active learning and other approaches. Chapter 5 suggests ways to help kids grow in faith through active learning.

● **Crafts**—Find creative people to lead children in making

WORKSHEET

Vacation Bible School Registration Card

Child's name _____

Child's address _____

City _____ State _____ ZIP _____

Telephone _____

Child's age _____ Child's birthdate _____

Name of person to contact in case of an emergency _____

Phone number of the person _____

Child's allergies _____

Any medical information about the child we need to know _____
_____

Is your child up-to-date on immunizations? _____

If not, which immunizations does your child need? _____

If you grant permission for your child to participate in vacation Bible school and release the church of any liability in case an accident occurs, sign and date below. _____

                                                    Signature and date

—J.R.—

CREATIVE IDEA

Attracting VBS Volunteers

Many adults would like to volunteer, but they have a problem: young children. Consider having a nursery to care for the infants of volunteers. That's what we do. We offer this service only for the volunteers, however, not for other parents who don't help and just want their young children to receive free care.

—M.P.—

innovative crafts. I recommend either one of the following two methods for doing crafts.

1. Have a craft theme that children can work on throughout the week and complete the last day. For example, one church had children work on a raised-relief clay model of Noah and the ark.

2. Have children complete a craft each day. Chapter 7 suggests many different craft techniques that can be useful in a VBS setting.

● **Refreshments**—Usually snacks consist of either store-bought or homemade cookies. But be creative in tying your refreshments to your VBS theme. For example, if you have a circus theme, consider serving frozen tiger milk (which is actually vanilla ice cream!).

● **Games**—Have games that fit with your VBS theme. Or just schedule a part of your program for children to play and have fun. See chapter 6 for game ideas.

Planning Your Vacation Bible School

When should you start planning for VBS? It really begins as soon as one is over. At this time you're fresh with ideas for the next time—how to improve, different approaches, problems you encountered and so forth.

Then, about six months in advance, enlist a VBS coordinator. This person can help recruit teachers and helpers. If you anticipate lots of kids, form committees for each of the vacation Bible school ingredients listed earlier in this chapter.

Three months before the event, start advertising for volunteers. Order VBS materials including curriculum, crafts and prizes.

Two months before the program, begin promoting the VBS.

WORKSHEET

A Vacation Bible School Checklist

12 months in advance:
- ☐ Set date.
- ☐ Request and evaluate sample curriculum from several publishers.

8 months in advance:
- ☐ Choose a theme.
- ☐ Order curriculum.

6 months in advance:
- ☐ Enlist a VBS coordinator.
- ☐ Form committees, if necessary.
- ☐ Design activities, crafts, snacks and lessons that fit the theme.
- ☐ List supplies you'll need.
- ☐ Book special guests, such as speakers, clowns, musicians or other performers.

3 months in advance:
- ☐ Order or purchase supplies.
- ☐ Recruit volunteers to teach, make snacks, coordinate crafts, lead music and take other leadership roles.

2 months in advance:
- ☐ Promote the vacation Bible school in the church and community.
- ☐ Train volunteers.
- ☐ Choose rooms for classes and activities.

3 weeks in advance:
- ☐ Meet with the custodian or appropriate person regarding setup and cleanup.
- ☐ Arrange for registration.
- ☐ Mail information to prospective families whose children aren't registered yet.

1 week in advance:
- ☐ Meet with volunteers to cover any last-minute details.

After the vacation Bible school:
- ☐ Write notes to children and volunteers.
- ☐ Evaluate the VBS, noting ideas that worked and ways to improve next year's program.

—M.P.—

Attract kids' attention with materials that set the mood for the theme you've chosen. For example, if you use the circus theme, attach helium balloons to posters and displays.

Also begin working with teachers to prepare materials for the week. Talk through learning objectives and approaches. Build a sense of community, teamwork and mutual trust among the leaders.

Two to three weeks before your start date, make sure families that participated in previous years are aware of this year's program.

One week before the event, meet with volunteers. Answer any questions they may have. Make sure all the last-minute details are in place.

Then enjoy your creative, life-changing vacation Bible school!

What Starts When VBS Ends

Yes, it's wise to start planning for next year's vacation Bible school when this year's ends. But you have more to do than that.

One week after our vacation Bible school, we mail a thank-you letter to each child for attending. Two weeks after the event, we have people visit each family that doesn't belong to our church. We bring a packet to each family with information about the congregation and our church's children's ministry, a Bible coloring book, crayons and stickers.

This is a low-pressure visit that gives the child fun activities to do and thanks the parents for allowing the child to attend. This visit gives parents a good impression of the church and may encourage them to visit.

But these visits still aren't the end. Throughout the year, we offer special events and invite all the VBS kids. For example we have a Great Pumpkin Pie Reunion and a Jingle-Jangle Jamboree that coincide with school holidays. Through these special events, children who usually don't attend your church keep coming back. And these events create excitement for your VBS program all year!

Vacation Bible school is an important part of your children's ministry. What a great way for children to learn more about God and experience that learning is fun!

CHAPTER 20

SUCCESSFUL AFTER-SCHOOL PROGRAMS

■ ■ ■ ■ ■ ■ ■ ■ ■ ■ ■ ■ ■ ■ ■

BY ELAINE FRIEDRICH

S chool hallways suddenly boil with rushing Reeboks and flying book bags when the last school bell rings for the day. A giggling hoard of children bursts through the school doors, happy that school's out.

Where are these kids running? Too many children head to empty houses after school because their parents work.

But today some kids are rushing to cars, not the buses they usually take. They're not headed home. They're off to a church for a special after-school program. Our church has found this to be an invaluable ministry opportunity. And we try to offer a fun, challenging after-school program kids love.

Starting (or improving) an after-school program doesn't need to be a complicated process. Here are nine steps I use:

Step 1: Determine the Need

Determine the needs of your church, children and community. If children don't need an after-school program, why have one? By surveying parents, teachers and others in the community, we can determine what needs are not currently being met and how the church might be able to minister to those needs.

Step 2: Determine Your Program's Purpose

Why start an after-school program? In our church, only 10 children showed up for children's choir in the afternoons. Kids didn't seem interested and involved. So to provide a ministry that would make a difference in kids' lives and provide an important service to families, we created an exciting after-school program. Our objective was to meet kids' spiritual and social needs at the same time.

What do we hope to accomplish? Our children's ministry program has four primary goals:

1. To develop adult discipleship,
2. To develop discipleship among children,
3. To strengthen families, and
4. To develop leaders.

We evaluate all our programs against these four goals. When we looked at our after-school program, Noah's Arts, we determined it accomplished the discipleship development of children through Bible study, music and building relationships with adults who model the Christian faith.

What kind of programs do churches offer for children during the week? In a survey of more than 1,500 churches having day-care centers, researchers learned the percentage of these churches that offer the following programs:

● Preschool program—95 percent
● Care of handicapped children—64 percent
● Toddler program—45 percent
● Before- or after-school program—29 percent
● Infant program—29 percent
● Mothers program—28 percent[1]

WORKSHEET

After-School Child-Care Questionnaire

Our church is trying to determine whether we should start an after-school program. Please complete the following questionnaire.

1. How many adults live in your home? _____

2. How many adults are employed outside of the home? _____

3. How many children do you have? _____

4. What are the ages of your children? _____

5. Do you currently use after-school child care? _____ If not, please skip to question #10.

6. Which of the following best describes your child's after-school arrangements?

☐ Child is at home with a parent.
☐ Child attends a day-care center (name of center: _____).
☐ Child stays with a sitter at home.
☐ Child stays home alone.
☐ Child stays home with siblings.
☐ Other (specify) _____.

7. Are you happy with your current after-school care? Why or why not?
_____

8. What type of programs does your current child-care service provide? (Check all that apply.)

☐ Tutoring   ☐ Recreation
☐ Art   ☐ Television viewing
☐ Lessons in music, dance, etc.   ☐ Spiritual training
☐ Other (specify) _____

9. What transportation is provided from school to the child-care center?

☐ No transportation is provided   ☐ A van or bus
☐ Parents car pool   ☐ A parent picks up the child
                                 ☐ Other:

10. Would you be interested in a child-care program if it were offered at this church? _____

11. Would you be willing to share in the leadership of the after-school child-care center if a need for this program is determined? _____

12. Your name _____

Address _____

City _____ State _____ ZIP _____

Day telephone _____ Evening telephone _____

—E.F.—

Step 3: Plan, Plan, Plan

The old expression is true: "If you fail to plan, you plan to fail." So decide who will design, develop and make decisions about your new program. The biggest mistake children's ministers make when they're planning new programs is getting a late start. It's impossible to pull off a quality, wide-scale ministry with inadequate lead time. I recommend you start planning nine to 12 months in advance.

It's wise to begin small and grow slowly. We started with 40 kids three years ago, and now we have 70. The smaller the group, the easier it is to correct the flaws and work out the kinks in the program.

Step 4: Choose a Focus

What will happen at your after-school program? Will it provide fellowship, tutoring, Bible study, arts and crafts, opportunities for service, music or a combination of these elements? These choices will depend on the specific needs you uncovered in step 1, plus the people, facilities and budget available.

Our Noah's Arts program offers recreation, arts and crafts, Bible study and music. Other ministries could include service projects, sports, tutoring and small-group Bible studies, depending on the needs and interests in your community.

Will you let children watch television? We intentionally don't use television in our programming. We want children to develop relationships with others, play basketball and other sports and do arts and crafts. Children can watch television at home.

Step 5: Decide Who Can Participate

Our after-school program is open to first- through fifth-graders, but the primary participants are first- through third-graders. Decide on a target age range for your program.

Also, decide whether children from other churches and from the community at large will be invited. Our program is open to everyone, regardless of church affiliation. Of the 70 children who

IN-DEPTH INFORMATION

Kids With Nothing to Do After School

The National Education Association reports that 2.1 million kids across the country go home to an empty house after school. That number is about equal to the entire combined population of Wyoming, Alaska, North Dakota and South Dakota.

When child development researcher Hyman Rodman surveyed 709 kids, he found many are alone after school. The percentage of kids who go home to an empty house:

- 50 percent of 9-year-olds
- 70 percent of 10-year-olds
- 82 percent of 11-year-olds
- 76 percent of 12-year-olds[2]

—J.R.—

attend our program, about 15 are unchurched kids. Many of them have now started coming to Sunday school, and they've motivated their parents to attend at the same time.

However, because of state standards, we're limited to a specific enrollment. We initially opened registration to church members up to a certain date. Any remaining openings were available for children from the community.

Step 6: Set a Regular Schedule

Tailor your program's schedule to meet the needs of the kids you're targeting. Decide what days and hours to operate.

Our church serves children from 55 elementary schools. Those schools dismiss any time from 2:30 p.m. to 4 p.m. Our program has to be flexible enough to allow for different schedules.

So we start our program at 3 p.m. with a recreation time in our gym. Kids can come any time up until 4:15 p.m. without missing anything. During that time, they can skate, play basketball or hockey and generally unwind. Snacks are also available.

At 4:30, all children leave the gym and walk across the street to the church building to participate in Bible instruction, choir and art activities. The program ends at 6 p.m.

Step 7: Develop a Transportation Plan

If your church has vans or buses, consider providing pick-up service. Or work out a car-pool plan with parents. We have many families who share transportation responsibilities. When parents register, we give them each a list of parents' addresses and phone numbers. They arrange their own car pools.

But try to arrange some type of transportation. According to parents surveyed by the Center for Early Adolescence, safety is the #1 barrier preventing parents from letting their children attend after-school programs.[3] If parents don't feel their children can safely get to the program, children won't come.

Step 8: Find Committed Leaders

First, decide whether you'll seek volunteers or paid professionals to staff your program. If you include volunteers, set their length of service. Six months to a year is reasonable.

We use both paid staff and volunteers in our Noah's Arts program, with the paid staff having major responsibility for coordinating the program. Each person has a specific responsibility, and teamwork is the key to our effectiveness.

Step 9: Evaluate Your Program

It's important to frequently ask yourself and your staff: How can we improve? For example, when we first started, children were crossing a busy, four-lane street from the gym to the church and back several times during the afternoon. We reorganized our programming so they cross the street only once.

Because the church has a significant message for the world, an after-school program can be a vehicle to share God's love with children. Our after-school ministry is growing because parents recognize the valuable Christian input their kids can receive.

Notes

■ ■ ■ ■

[1]Eileen W. Lindner, Mary C. Mattis, June R. Rogers, *When Churches Mind the Children* (Ypsilanti, MI: The High/Scope Press, 1983), 42.

[2]Jolene L. Roehlkepartain, "Home Alone," JR. HIGH MINISTRY Magazine, (March/April 1991), 16-17.

[3]Joan S. Lipsitz, *After School: Young Adolescents on Their Own* (Carrboro, NC: Center for Early Adolescence, 1986), 21.

CHAPTER 21

SPECIAL MINISTRIES FOR SPECIAL NEEDS

■ ■ ■ ■ ■ ■ ■ ■ ■ ■ ■ ■ ■ ■ ■ ■

BY WAYNE TESCH

A bout one in 20 children and teenagers in the United States has some sort of disability.[1] Yet many churches overlook these children and their needs. As a result, these children are rarely integrated into the church, and they become overlooked and forgotten.

There are multitudes of special needs that churches could address—physical disabilities, low-income children, developmentally disabled children and many more. This chapter focuses on three issues as "case studies" to introduce the broad range of needs and to give ideas for responding to the challenge of meeting the needs of *all* children.

Child Abuse and Neglect

The National Committee for Prevention of Child Abuse reports that 2.5 million children in the United States are abused or neglected.[2] And the numbers appear to be rising dramatically. In Orange County, California, for example, more than 15,000 mandated reports of child abuse were made in 1985. Five years later that figure had risen to more than 28,000.[3]

Children who are abused and neglected usually go unnoticed because our society has learned so well how to mask the effects of abuse. Children sit in our classes trying to hear what's being taught. But because of the abuse and pain in their lives, they don't "hear" the message of love and hope.

Abuse and neglect are serious issues that must be taken seriously. When you suspect that a child may be neglected or physically, sexually or emotionally abused, report your suspicion to your state's child protection agency.

If you don't report your suspicion, you could be held liable. Most states require children's workers to contact the county social services agency in cases of known or suspected abuse.

To find out the laws in your state, call Child Protection Services. Find it in the government section of your telephone book under your city or county name. Then look under the Department of Social Services for Child Protection Services.

You may also want to notify your senior pastor, but don't tell the family or other church members involved. If your suspicion is unfounded, you could start ugly, false rumors. And if your suspicion is true, you could alienate people and miss opportunities to help by spreading the information beyond the professionals who need to know.

How can we minister to abused and neglected children? Many ministries are possible, including counseling and other services for children who have been discovered to be abused and neglected. Ministries to support families going through this kind of trauma could also be appropriate.

One positive, pro-active ministry would be to teach a body safety program in which children learn the importance of protecting their bodies and what's inappropriate for others to do to them. Schools teach fire safety, home safety, driver education and first aid. Your church could teach self-protection skills to children.

The Center for the Prevention of Sexual and Domestic Violence, an interreligious educational ministry in Seattle, has developed a child sexual abuse curriculum for churches to use with 9- to 12-year-olds. The curriculum includes 13 sessions with topics such as "God Wants You to Be Safe," "Saying 'No!' " and "Good Touch/Bad Touch/Confusing Touch."[4]

Hospitalized Children

I recall sitting in the doctor's office with my wife when he told us there was a mass behind the eye socket of our 8-year-old daughter. Our hearts raced! What was wrong?

After seeing a specialist, we found Renée had a bone disorder called fibrous dysplasia. Since her first hospital visit, she's had two additional major surgeries on her sinus cavity. That experience has given us new insight into ministering to children in the hospital.

● Encourage parents of potential pediatric patients to tour the facility ahead of time. Walking through the hospital helps prepare the child and the parents.

Before our daughter went to the hospital, we took one of these tours. Renée tried on a wristband like she'd wear when she was hospitalized. We sampled cafeteria food. Our daughter received a first-aid kit. We walked through the admitting procedure. And we observed other children playing in the playroom.

● Prepare the child spiritually. Read scriptures to the child that will encourage the child. Twelve years after the hospital visits, our daughter's favorite scripture still is Joshua 1:9. "Have I not commanded you? Be strong and courageous. Do not be terrified; do not be discouraged, for the Lord your God will be with you

---

CREATIVE IDEA

10 Ways to Brighten a Hospital Stay

1. Send cards to let the child know you're praying for him or her.
2. Volunteer to clean the house for the parents.
3. Mow the lawn for the family.
4. Take meals to the house during the child's recovery.
5. Collect offerings to help if the family's expenses are high.
6. Provide transportation back and forth to the hospital.
7. Babysit the child's siblings.
8. Provide guest rooms for relatives who fly or drive in.
9. Give the child Play-Doh or Silly Putty. A child can release a lot of nervous energy by squeezing, squashing and pinching Play-Doh or Silly Putty.
10. Read aloud the child's favorite stories.

—W.T.—

wherever you go." That's the one we read to her before she went into the hospital.

● Encourage children to take a favorite stuffed animal to the hospital. Renée's favorite elephant went through surgery with her. The nurses put a wristband on "Elephanté" and placed a surgical mask and cap on him. Stuffed animals say, "We care; we're thinking of you."

● Have the child's Sunday school class prepare an activity basket for the child. Include small items the child can open each day. Depending on the child's age, good gifts might be a Slinky, a Gumby character, word-game books, crayons and coloring books.

Developmentally Disabled Children

One Sunday afternoon when I was growing up, I couldn't find my younger brother, Gary. Racing through our second floor apartment, I searched every room. When I looked out the open back door, I saw my 14-month-old brother at the bottom of the steps. He was bleeding and motionless on the concrete landing.

After a couple of weeks in the hospital, Gary came home. But he was different. Later we learned he had a brain injury, rendering him "mentally retarded."

A ministry for the developmentally disadvantaged can be patterned after the model in Nehemiah 1—6 where Nehemiah did the impossible: he rebuilt the walls of Jerusalem in 52 days.

To do this, first identify the need. For Nehemiah, the agony of having Jerusalem's walls in ruins caused him to sit and cry—and then respond. Like Nehemiah, listen to the needs around you. Ask yourself: What breaks my heart? Then ask yourself what your children's ministry is doing about it.

Then pray. And when you're finished, pray more—like Nehemiah did. Our children's ministry will become more effective when we communicate often with God. During times of prayer, our minds become more receptive to God's voice.

Whenever we attempt a new ministry, especially to reach children with special needs, problems will arise. People will say: "It can't be done!" "Are you crazy?" or "Are you sure this is what God wants you to do?"

IN-DEPTH INFORMATION

Mentally Disabled Children

Experts categorize mentally disabled children into three types: educable, trainable and profoundly disabled. Here's a brief description of each.

	EDUCABLE	TRAINABLE	PROFOUND
IQ Range	55-79	35-55	Below 30
Percent of retarded population	84%	13%	3%
Description	Able to learn, and progresses slowly	Able to learn self-help skills, social-ization and simple household chores.	Has minimal capacity to learn.
Academic achievement	Can learn to read, write, do math computa-tions.	Can learn to recognize his or her name. May be able to print name and address.	May respond in minimal ways to training.
Social achievement	Can learn to live independently in a community.	Can learn to be-have properly. Can't live inde-pendently.	Has limited social skills.
Occupation potential	Can work in jobs requiring limited cognitive skills.	Can work only in a specially equipped workshop.	Requires complete care and supervision.[5]

—W.T.—

WORKSHEET

Test Your Ministry Readiness

Before you begin working with disabled children, make sure you're trained and ready. Ask yourself:

	Yes	No
Have parents each filled out a brief health form that includes information about the child's allergies, medical conditions and activities that should be limited?	☐	☐
Have you taken a first-aid course?	☐	☐
Are you certified in CPR?	☐	☐
Have you contacted an agency dealing with the specific disability for information on how to work with the child?	☐	☐
Have you sought advice from experts or other people doing similar ministries?	☐	☐
Have you watched someone else working with these children?	☐	☐
Have you taken a class on the disability through the community center, hospital or local college?	☐	☐
Have you recruited volunteers who have training?	☐	☐

The more yes boxes you checked, the more prepared you are.

—T.V.—

When doubts come, remember listening to God's voice. Each hurdle is an opportunity to see God's creative power at work.

A Touching Ministry

As you begin to minister to children with special needs, you'll touch entire families who need the reassurance of God's love. Families will greatly appreciate a church that ministers to their special children. And as you minister to the child, you'll soon be ministering to the entire family.

IN-DEPTH INFORMATION

Helpful Organizations

Don't go it alone in ministering to children with special needs. These organizations will give you more information and support.

Organization	What the Organization Offers
Children's Defense Fund 122 C St. N.W., Ste. 400 Washington, DC 20001 (202) 628-8787	Resources and advocacy for children.
For Kids Sake, Inc. Box 313 Lake Elsinore, CA 92331-0313 (714) 244-9001	Resources and workshops. Parenting and child-safety education.
C. Henry Kempe National Center for Prevention and Treatment of Child Abuse and Neglect 1205 Oneida St. Denver, CO 80220 (303) 321-3963	Family evaluation program. In-depth evaluation of family for court or treatment recommendations. Preschool for sexually abused children. Extensive library of audiovisuals and publications.
National Committee for Prevention of Child Abuse 332 S. Michigan Ave. Ste. 1600 Chicago, IL 60604-4357 (312) 663-3520	Programs on public awareness, education and prevention of child abuse.
Royal Family Kids' Camps, Inc. 1068 Salinas Ave. Costa Mesa, CA 92626 (714) 556-1420	Mobilization of churches to reach abused and neglected children in their own communities.
Society's League Against Molesters (SLAM) Box 346 Collingswood, NJ 08108 (609) 858-7800	Lobbying against child molesters. Monitoring and evaluation of courtrooms. Sponsorship of meetings to educate the public.

—W.T.—

Notes

■ ■ ■ ■

[1] *The Youth Ministry Resource Book*, edited by Eugene C. Roehlkepartain (Loveland, CO: Group Books, 1988), 157.

[2] Deborah Mesce, "More Child Abuse Cases Being Reported," Orange County Register (April 17, 1991).

[3] "Child Abuse Registry Reports, 1985-1990," Social Services Administration, Orange County, CA.

[4] Kathryn Goering Reid with Marie M. Fortune, *Preventing Child Sexual Abuse* (New York: Pilgrim Press, 1989).

[5] Gene Newman and Joni Eareckson Tada, *All God's Children: Ministry to the Disabled* (Grand Rapids, MI: Zondervan, 1981), 43.

CHILDREN'S DEVELOPMENTAL STAGES AND NEEDS

■ ■ ■ ■ ■ ■ ■ ■ ■ ■ ■ ■ ■ ■ ■ ■

BY JOLENE L. ROEHLKEPARTAIN

Between the ages of 3 and 12, children race through an array of developmental steps. The following chart highlights only a few of these for each age group. Chapters 10 to 14 give more in-depth information about ministry to specific age groups.

3-YEAR-OLDS

Physically	Emotionally	Spiritually	Socially	Intellectually
• Move constantly; develop large muscles with walking, running • Have bursts of energy and then tire easily • Develop hand skills with activities such as building with blocks	• Act at a feeling level • Respond to emotions adults display • Are becoming sensitive to the way others act	• Understand spontaneous prayer, not formal prayer • Understand God's love by the way parents love them • Understand God by the way people treat each other rather than by what people say about God	• Prefer to play alone • Lack social skills; may push another child to get the child to play • Self-centered; need training in cooperation and taking turns	• Don't understand any symbolism • Understand only one direction at a time • Have a limited attention span, usually around three minutes

4-YEAR-OLDS

Physically	Emotionally	Spiritually	Socially	Intellectually
• Coordination improves; begin jumping, climbing, skipping • Small muscles begin to develop; learn to tie shoe laces, button, zip • Are active but tire easily; may kick or hit others	• Develop a sense of humor • Are sensitive to adults' moods and actions • Test limits and rules; throw tantrums	• Understand that praying means talking to God • Understand God's love by the way others express love to them • Ask questions about God	• Seek the approval of adults • Want to spend more time with others and less time by themselves • Do a lot of imaginary play experiences with other children	• Have short attention spans; sit quietly for about four minutes • Are curious; ask "how," "what" and "why" frequently • Learn by doing and experiencing their five senses

5-YEAR-OLDS

Physically
- Are more coordinated, agile and strong
- Need lots of room to run, hop, jump and move around
- Develop hand skills; can cut large objects and almost color within the lines

Emotionally
- Thrive on the attention of other peers and adults
- Feel proud when praised for doing something well
- Feel self-conscious when compared to other children

Spiritually
- Understand God made them
- Articulate God's love by doing kind things to others
- Notice when adults say one thing about God and then act differently

Socially
- Tattle to get attention
- Prefer playing with two or three children instead of large groups
- Want to play games other kids are playing or mimic activities that adults do

Intellectually
- Have an attention span of about five minutes
- Can carry out instructions
- Triple their vocabularies within one year, from about 1,500 words at age 4 to 5,000 words at age 5

GRADES 1 AND 2

Physically
- Enjoy active play such as jumping and running
- Experience a slowing in rapid growth
- Develop small muscle coordination; begin to write

Emotionally
- Express feelings with physical action; may hit others
- Crave attention
- Are self-centered; each child wants to be first

Spiritually
- Sense God's love and God's world by personal experience
- Are baffled by the fact they can't see God
- Don't comprehend the Bible's chronology except that the Old Testament came before Jesus and the New Testament talks about Jesus

Socially
- Usually tolerate kids from different racial and economic backgrounds
- Want to please teachers
- Want to win and always be first

Intellectually
- Interested in concrete learning experiences such as dramatizations and rhythms
- Can sit still for about six to seven minutes
- Have a limited concept of time and space; are interested in the present, not in the past or future

GRADES 3 AND 4

Physically	Emotionally	Spiritually	Socially	Intellectually
• Develop speed and accuracy in playing games • Girls develop faster than boys, especially in small-muscle skills • Play with lots of repetition to develop skills	• Easily become frustrated because of trying to do activities that are beyond them developmentally • Vent anger by teasing or criticizing others • Have difficulty accepting constructive criticism	• Want God's help and guidance • Want to become part of God's family but don't completely understand the concept of a personal savior • Question how God answers prayer	• Want to fit in and belong to a peer group • Want to play with members of the same sex • Begin to be less dependent on adults	• Can sit still for about eight to nine minutes • Can accurately group and classify information • Ask in-depth questions instead of simple questions

GRADES 5 AND 6

Physically	Emotionally	Spiritually	Socially	Intellectually
• Grow in bone structure, making bones susceptible to injury • Differ in growth rates by gender; girls forge ahead of boys in height and weight; some girls may get their menstrual periods • Prefer same-sex activities since girls are developing faster than boys, and boys prefer to play rougher than girls	• Are emotionally more balanced; tend to be more easygoing • Are becoming more self-conscious • Base feelings on how others respond to them	• Begin to understand biblical symbolism • Tell friends about God when excited about God • Want to attend church; want to do service projects	• Become interested in competition—but not in competition that points out the differences between them and their peers • Want peers to play fair; become upset when others break rules • Develop individual leadership qualities	• Can usually sit still for 10 to 11 minutes, although some children can become absorbed in a project that interests them • Can think to themselves, causing communication to drop off • Develop a wider range of interests

RESOURCES FOR CHILDREN'S MINISTRY

■ ■ ■ ■ ■ ■ ■ ■ ■ ■ ■ ■ ■ ■ ■

Adventures in Creative Teaching by Elsiebeth McDaniel (Wheaton, IL: Victor Books, 1986).

Basic Skills for Church Teachers by Donald L. Griggs (Nashville, TN: Abingdon Press, 1985).

Basic Teacher Skills: Handbook for Church School Teachers by Richard E. Rusbuldt (Valley Forge, PA: Judson Press, 1981).

Biblical Puppet Performances by Judith Campuano-Schera, Joan Minardi-Harniman, and Phyllis A. Narducci-Gargano (Carthage, IL: Shining Star Publications, 1990).

A Celebration of Notes, Book 1 by Jane Smisor Bastien (San Diego; Neil A. Kjos Music Company, 1990).

Children Belong in Worship: A Guide to the Children's Sermon by W. Alan Smith (St. Louis: CBP Press, 1984).

Children in the Worshipping Community by David Ng and Virginia Thomas (Louisville, KY: Westminster John Knox, 1981).

Children's Church: A Comprehensive How-To by Doris A. Freese (Chicago: Moody Press, 1982).

Children's Ministry Clip Art by Mary Lynn Ulrich (Loveland, CO: Group Books, 1990).

CHILDREN'S MINISTRY Magazine published bimonthly, Box 442, Mt. Morris, IL 61054.

Clown Ministry by Floyd Shaffer and Penne Sewall (Loveland, CO: Group Books, 1984).

Clown Ministry Skits for All Seasons by Floyd Shaffer (Loveland, CO: Group Books, 1990).

Color by Interval by Sharon Kaplan (Hialeah, FL: CPP/Belwin, Inc., 1989).

Cooperative Discipline Teacher's Guide by Linda Albert (Circle Pines, MN: American Guidance Service, 1990).

The Cooperative Sports & Games Book by Terry Orlick (New York: Pantheon Books, 1978).

Creative Art for the Developing Child by Clare Cherry (Belmont, CA: Fearon Teacher Aids, 1990).

Creative Christian Education: Teaching the Bible Through the Church Year by Howard Hanchey (Wilton, CT: Morehouse-Barlow, 1986).

The Developing Person Through Childhood and Adolescence by Kathleen Stassen Berger (New York: Worth Publishers, Inc., 1986).

Everything You Want to Know About Teaching Children, Grades 1-6 by Barbara Bolton, Charles T. Smith and Wes Haystead (Ventura, CA: Gospel Light Publications, 1987).

Everything You Want to Know About Teaching Young Children, Birth-6 Years by Wesley Haystead (Ventura, CA: Gospel Light Publications, 1989).

Experiencing the Bible With Children by Dorothy Jean Furnish (Nashville, TN: Abingdon Press, 1990).

Exploring Christian Education Effectiveness by Eugene C. Roehlkepartain (Minneapolis: Search Institute, 1990).

Faith-Building Meetings for Upper-Elementary Kids by various authors (Loveland, CO: Group Books, 1991).

Five-Minute Bible Fun, Lesson Openers by Elizabeth Whitney Crisci (Carthage, IL: Shining Star Publications, 1991).

Free and Inexpensive Teaching Tools by Pat Loring (Carthage, IL: Good Apple, Inc., 1986).

Fun Group Games for Children's Ministry by various authors (Loveland, CO: Group Books, 1990).

Guide for Ministry With Elementary Children by Lee Miller

(Memphis, TN: Board of Christian Education, Cumberland Presbyterian Church, 1988).

Guide for Ministry With Young Children by Ann Schroer (Memphis, TN: Board of Christian Education, Cumberland Presbyterian Church, 1988).

Harper's Encyclopedia of Religious Education edited by Iris V. Cully and Kendig Brubaker Cully (New York: Harper & Row, 1990).

How To Do Bible Learning Activities, Grades 1-6, Book 1 by Barbara Bolton (Ventura, CA: Gospel Light Publications, 1982).

How To Do Bible Learning Activities, Grades 1-6, Book 2 by Barbara Bolton (Ventura, CA: Gospel Light Publications, 1984).

How to Guide Preschoolers compiled by Jenell Strickland (Nashville, TN: Convention Press, 1982).

The Hurried Child: Growing Up Too Fast Too Soon by David Elkind (Reading, MA: Addison-Wesley Publishing, 1989).

I Can Make a Rainbow by Marjorie Frank (Bronx, NY: Incentive Publishing, 1976).

I Have Something to Say about This Big Trouble: Children of the Tenderloin Speak Out collected by Reverend Cecil Williams and Janice Mirikitani (San Francisco: Glide Word Press, 1989).

Lively Bible Lessons for Grades K-3 by various authors (Loveland, CO: Group Books, 1991).

Lively Bible Lessons for Preschoolers by various authors (Loveland, CO: Group Books, 1991).

Mime Ministry by Susan Kelly Toomey (Colorado Springs, CO: Meriwether Publishing, 1986).

More New Games and Playful Ideas by Andrew Fluegelman (New York: Doubleday, 1981).

National Association for the Education of Young Children, 1834 Connecticut Ave. N.W., Washington, D.C. 20009-5786.

The New Games Book edited by Andrew Fluegelman (New York: Doubleday, 1976).

New Games for the Whole Family by Dale N. LeFevre (New York: Putnam, 1988).

Note Designs: A Coloring Note Speller by Jane Smisor Bastien (San Diego: Neil A. Kjos Music Company, 1989).

Object Talks from A to Z by Carol DeWolf (Cincinnati: Standard Publishing, 1987).

On Tablets of Human Hearts by Mary Ellen Drushal (Grand Rapids, MI: Zondervan, 1990).

Opening the Bible with Children: Beginning Bible Schools by Patricia Griggs (Nashville, TN: Abingdon Press, 1986).

Playfair: Everybody's Guide to Noncompetitive Play by Matt Weinstein and Joel Goodman (San Luis Obispo, CA: Impact Publishers, 1980).

Preschool Director's Survival Guide by Rebecca Graff (Englewood Cliffs, NJ: Prentice Hall, Center for Applied Research, 1990).

Preschool Handbook: A Guide to Organizing Preschool Programs by Mary Irene Flanagan (New York: Harper & Row, 1990).

Puppets: Ministry Magic by Dale and Liz VonSeggen (Loveland, CO: Group Books, 1990).

Quick Group Devotions for Children's Ministry by various contributors (Loveland, CO: Group Books, 1990).

The Quicksilver Years: The Hopes and Fears of Early Adolescence by Peter L. Benson, Dorothy Williams and Arthur Johnson (New York: Harper & Row, 1986).

Ready, Set . . . Sing! edited by Mary M. Nicol and Pamela M. Roth (Valley Forge, PA: Judson Press, 1989).

Scribble Cookies and Other Independent Creative Art Experiences for Children by MaryAnn F. Kohl (Bellingham, WA: Bright Ring Publishing, 1985).

The Second Cooperative Sports & Games Book by Terry Orlick (New York: Pantheon Books, 1982).

The Secret Life of the Unborn Child by Thomas Verny, M.D. with John Kelly (New York: Dell Publishing, 1982).

Seven Things Children Need by John M. Drescher (Scottsdale, PA: Herald Press, 1988).

Sing 'n' Celebrate for Kids by various songwriters (Irving, TX: Word Inc., 1977).

Something More: Nurturing Your Child's Spiritual Growth by Jean Grasso Fitzpatrick (New York: Viking, 1991).

The Spiritual Life of Children by Robert Coles (Boston: Houghton Mifflin, Co., 1990).

The State of America's Children: 1991 (Washington, DC: Children's Defense Fund, 1991).

A Summary Report on Faith, Loyalty, and Congregational Life by Peter L. Benson and Carolyn H. Eklin (Minneapolis: Search Institute, 1990).

Sunday School Standards by Lowell E. Brown (Ventura, CA: Gospel Light Publications, 1986).

Sunday Sing-A-Long (Volumes 1-4); Bible Song Sing-A-Long (Volumes 1 & 2); Kids Sing-A-Long Hymns; and *Kids Christmas Sing-A-Long* cassettes (Costa Mesa, CA: Maranatha! Music).

Teaching Your Child About God by Wes Haystead (Ventura, CA: Regal Books, 1983).

Upper-Elementary Meetings by various authors (Loveland, CO: Group Books, 1989).

Ways to Plan and Organize Your Sunday School: Early Childhood Birth-5 Years by Wesley Haystead (Glendale, CA: Gospel Light Publications, 1971).

Welcome the Child: A Child Advocacy Guide for Churches by Kathleen A. Guy (Washington, DC: Children's Defense Fund, 1991).

When Churches Mind the Children by Eileen W. Lindner, Mary C. Mattis and June R. Rogers (Ypsilanti, MI: The High/Scope Press, 1983).

CONTRIBUTORS

■ ■ ■ ■ ■ ■ ■ ■ ■ ■ ■ ■ ■ ■ ■ ■

Vicki Ashcraft is involved in prenatal ministry in New Mexico. She has 16 years experience as a children's minister and workshop leader.

Linda Becken is an administrator and teacher of an early childhood program in Wisconsin. She has worked with children for 18 years.

Rick Chromey is a minister of family life in Missouri. He has worked with children for eight years and is author of *Youth Ministry in Small Churches*.

Jean Cozby is a director of nursery ministries in Washington. She has worked with children for over 20 years.

Mary Irene Flanagan, C.S.J., is an early childhood and family minister, responsible for a large preschool program in California. She has been in children's ministry for 38 years. She is the author of *Preschool Handbook, Me at Three* and *Me at Four* among other books.

Lisa Flinn is a former public school teacher and curriculum developer in North Carolina. She has worked with children for 12 years and is the co-author of *Food for Christian Thought*.

Elaine Friedrich is the director of an elementary ministry in Texas. She has worked with children for 12 years.

Wes Haystead is an editorial director in California. He has worked with children for 30 years. He is the author of numerous books, including *Touching Tomorrow by Teaching Children,*

Everything You Want to Know About Teaching Young Children and *Teaching Your Child About God.*

Margaret Rickers Hinchey is a director of music in Colorado. She has been involved in children's music ministry for 17 years.

Vince Isner is a writer, producer, speaker and workshop leader in Tennessee. He has worked with children for 14 years.

Mitchell Picard is a children's pastor in Pennsylvania. He has worked with children for 13 years. He is the author of *Magical Messages* and *Kids, Sermons and Things.*

Earl Radford is a minister for children in California. He has worked with children for 15 years.

Jolene L. Roehlkepartain is a contributing editor for CHILDREN'S MINISTRY Magazine who lives in Minnesota. She has worked with children for six years.

Mary Gray Swan is a director of Christian education in Texas. She has worked with children for 20 years. She has published denominational church curriculum for children.

Wayne Tesch is founder and director of Royal Family Kids Camp. He has worked with children for 18 years.

Terry Vermillion is a workshop leader and former director of a preschool program in Missouri. She has worked with children for 20 years. She is a contributor to *Upper-Elementary Meetings, Fun Group Games for Children's Ministry* and *Quick Group Devotions for Children's Ministry.*

Dale and Liz VonSeggen are children's ministry consultants and trainers based in Colorado. They've worked with children for 25 years. They've written more than 200 puppet and ventriloquism scripts, and are authors of *Puppets: Ministry Magic.*

Paul E. White, Ph. D. is a child and family therapist in Kansas. He has worked with children for 10 years.

Dan Wiard is a Christian educator in Pennsylvania. He has worked with children for 10 years.

Judy Wortley is a children's ministry consultant based in California. She has worked with children for 18 years. She is the author of *Recruiting Remedy* and *Training Remedy.*

Barbara Younger is a writer and former children's librarian. She has worked with children for 15 years, and is the co-author of *Food for Christian Thought.*

Dynamic Resources for Children's Ministry

Lively Bible Lessons for Preschoolers

edited by Cindy S. Hansen

Sunday school teachers and children's church workers will love these exciting Bible lessons that make learning meaningful while keeping it fun. Discover 20 easy-to-use lessons packed with tot-size activities designed especially for preschoolers.

Each prepare-in-a-flash lesson helps younger children explore important topics, such as ...

- how God takes care of them—even when they're afraid.
- why each of them is a special person.
- how to share—and care for others.
- the importance of being kind.
- ways Jesus is with them at all times.

You'll also find great games that grab kids' attention. Creative learning experiences that teach Bible truths. Fun crafts children will love. Simple songs that help kids remember. And more—including special lessons for Easter, birthdays, Thanksgiving and Christmas.

Help energize your ministry to younger kids with **Lively Bible Lessons for Preschoolers.**

ISBN 1-55945-067-3 $9.95

Lively Bible Lessons for Grades K-3

edited by Cindy S. Hansen

Lively Bible Lessons for Grades K-3 makes creative teaching a snap! You can choose from 20 complete lessons that are ready in minutes—and require only a few simple, easy-to-grab supplies!

Make learning the Bible fun for this active age group with pizazz-packed lessons that help children learn and remember ...

- how God helps them with their fears.
- the importance of helping others.
- why each person is special.
- how to be a good friend.
- who Jesus is—and what he did for them.

...plus, meaningful lessons for special celebrations—including Christmas. Birthdays. Thanksgiving. And Easter.

There are also tons of super snack ideas to keep kids content. Games that fire their excitement. Crafts to hold their interest. And songs that keep lessons fresh in their minds.

Lively Bible Lessons for Grades K-3 will give your children's ministry a real boost—with the proven strategies of experienced teachers from across the continent!

ISBN 1-55945-074-6 $9.95

Fun Group Games for Children's Ministry

from the editors of Group Books

Get 100 faith-building games to energize activities with elementary kids. Discover exciting games to ...

- Increase Bible knowledge
- Teach teamwork
- Experience cooperation
- Build group unity
- Have fun!

You'll also find ...

- Bible-learning games for communicating basic Bible knowledge
- Energy-burning games for helping kids settle down
- Games with a message for increasing kids' sensitivity toward others
- Fun group games for low- or no-competition activities everyone can play
- Relays for wild variations of the ever-popular race
- Teamwork-builders for helping kids learn to cooperate with one another

These 100 games provide endless options for use in Sunday school, meetings, parties, summer camps—wherever you have a group of kids. They're excellent crowdbreakers, energizers and boredom busters.

ISBN 1-55945-003-7 $8.95

Children's Ministry Clip Art

Mary Lynn Ulrich

Add pizazz and style to your ministry with **Children's Ministry Clip Art**. Use these lively illustrations in newsletters, fliers, letters and bulletin boards—anywhere you need to grab kids'—and parents'—attention.

With this creative art, you can ...

- Design fabulous fliers and handouts for meetings on dozens of topics
- Announce upcoming events with zany, attention-getting calendars
- Promote specific children's ministry programs

This giant collection of clip art will add a professional touch to your children's ministry. It's as easy as 1-2-3.

          1-Choose your art   2-Cut it out   3-Paste it down

and your publicity is ready to go!

ISBN 1-55945-018-5 $14.95

Available at your local Christian bookstore, or write: Group Books, Box 485, Loveland, CO 80539. Please add postage/handling of $3 for mail orders of up to $15, $4 for orders of $15.01+. Colorado residents add 3% sales tax.